HOW I BECAME A CHRISTIAN DESPITE THE CHURCH

Greg Austen

ENDORSEMENTS

"Greg has braved the intensely challenging and not-often traveled road of sorting out toxic childhood beliefs while retaining a strong faith in Jesus Christ. This candid account of his journey to spiritual freedom is a gut-wrenching read with a happy ending that will give hope to anyone navigating a similar path."

>—Alli Nielsen,
>Center Content Manager for Care Net
>Lansdowne, VA

"I've had the pleasure of calling Greg a friend and colleague in ministry for several years now. In that time I've benefitted greatly from his wisdom, Christian maturity and insightful perspectives. This book helps explain how the crucible of Greg's earlier life has made him the man and leader that he is today. As he tells his story, Greg offers a path of healing and restoration for others who might have experienced a similar journey to his own. Greg's adept use of culture to illustrate the narrative adds to the book, with even a suggested song playlist included! I, for one, am grateful for how Greg Austen became a Christian despite the Church…and for how this book can help many other people."

>—Andrew Smith,
>Pastor of Presbyterian Church of Kennett Square (EPC)
>Kennett Square, PA

"It's easy enough, when one has grown up in a religiously manipulative and abusive environment, to reject faith altogether. Indeed, bookstores are replete with such memoirs of former "saints" who have bid God farewell. This isn't one of those books. Greg shares intimate and painful stories of a childhood marred by religious abuse— abuse that left scars still felt today. Yet despite the hurt and pain, Greg chose a more difficult path. He chose to search his past for the love masked by the hurt and the truth behind all the lies. If you've been let down by the church, or been one of the many abused by it, this book will give you a glimpse into how one can still find God, even when most of what you've seen done in His name is anything but holy."

>—Ardee Coolidge,
>Leesburg Church of the Nazarene
>Leesburg, VA

"Dr. Austen has written an intensely personal narrative detailing the toxic effects on himself and his family of sinful and dysfunctional church leadership. While he is specific in describing the long term damage with which he still struggles, the theme of redemption is never absent. Gathering data from theology to pop culture, he demonstrates how a Biblical world view, and firm commitment to historic Christianity, provides hope and a measure of healing. Jesus said he would build his Church and hell would not overcome it. Dr. Austen proves that even the damage we inflict on the Body of Christ cannot stop God's work of grace in his children."

>—Dr. Ken Larter
>Pastor, Deerfield Presbyterian Church (EPC)
>Deerfield, NJ

Copyright © 2020 Greg Austen

All rights reserved.

No part of this book may be reproduced, or stored in a retrieval system, or transmitted in any form or by any means- electronic, mechanical, photocopying, recording, scanning or other- except for brief quotations in critical reviews or articles, without prior written permission of the publisher.

Published by Greg Austen through Kindle Direct Publishing.

ISBN-13: 9798617434493

Scripture quotations marked ESV are from THE ENGLISH STANDARD VERSION. @ 2001 Crossway Bibles, a division of Good News Publishers.

Scripture quotations marked KJV are from the King James Version.

Scripture quotations marked (NLT) are taken from the Holy Bible, New Living Translation, copyright © 1996, 2004, 2007 by Tyndale House Foundation. Used by permission of Tyndale House Publishers, Inc., Carol Stream, IL 60188. All rights reserved.

Scripture quotations marked as NIV are taken from the HOLY BIBLE, NEW INTERNATIONAL VERSION®. Copyright © 1973, 1978, 1984 Biblica. Used by permission of Zondervan. All rights reserved. The "NIV" and "New International Version" trademarks are registered in the United States Patent and Trademark Office by Biblica. Use of either trademark requires the permission of Biblica.

Scripture quotations marked NRSV are from the New Revised Standard Version Bible, copyright © 1989 the Division of Christian Education of the National Council of the Churches of Christ in the United States of America. Used by permission. All rights reserved.

Cover: *The Starry Night* (1889) by Vincent Van Gogh. Original from Wikimedia Commons. Digitally enhanced by rawpixel. Public domain Creative Commons image.

To my parents. I stand on your shoulders and I'm sorry for what you've suffered. May this unvarnished retelling of our story; albeit, through my eyes, be indelible proof to all who read that God doesn't waste pain.

I will build my church, and the gates of hell shall not prevail against it.[1]
—Jesus

The Starry Night by Vincent Van Gogh, the painting on the front cover, is one of the most recognized pieces of art in the world. Notice that, although the homes are lit with a warm glow, the steepled church—the primary entity designed to show God's love and light—is unlit. Many, like Vincent, have experienced church as soul-killing and light-diminishing. Still others have found it to be a place of great darkness as well. Indeed, this is my story…

Gratefully, however, it's not its end.

---

[1] Matthew 16:18b, ESV.

Table of Contents

INTRODUCTION 1
    Unique Take 3
    Constructive Tone 4

CHAPTER ONE: A RIVER RAN THROUGH IT 9
    Geographic Roots 11
    The Poor Parson and His Wife 12
    Formative Views of Sexuality 14
    The Double Helix of Faith and Family—Why it Matters 16
    The Double Helix Illustrated 19

CHAPTER TWO: GOD VERSUS THE BOULEVARD 23
    Tickets and Scalps 25
    Returning to "God Versus the Boulevard" 29
    More on Culture & the World 30
    Fun-suckers & Manipulators 33

CHAPTER THREE: SHAME, DISTORTIONS, AND ABUSE 37
    Shame 40
    Distorted Views of Sex 41
    Abuse 45

CHAPTER FOUR: BREAKING FREE 51
    Chess with My Grandfather 52
    A Girl Named Maria 53
    Heroes, Victims, and a Gift from My Dad 55
    The Jonestown Massacre 57

CHAPTER FIVE: HEALING MOVES 63
    Unexpected Love 64
    Wolves in Sheep's Clothing Exposed 65
    Shame and Repressed Memories 67
    Forgiveness 70
    Therapy 74

CHAPTER SIX: SEXUAL STAGGERS 77

Why Can't I Change? 79
The Christian Foundation for Sexual Healing 81
Five Strategies for Fighting Lust 83
Navigating Mid-life and the Empty Nest 86
Getting Our Apologetic Against Pornography Right 89

CHAPTER SEVEN: LEARNING TO LOVE 93
Managing Our Own Store 93
Not Pulling Back 95
Shame-based versus Grace-based Churches 99
How God Uses Our Kids 101
"Trembling on the Brink of Disaster" 102
Finding Ourselves 104

CHAPTER EIGHT: FINDING GOD 107
Why I Believe in a Loving Creator 107
Why I'm a Christian 110
Still Plenty of Questions 117
Hope and the Father Heart of God 119

CHAPTER NINE: WHY IT HAPPENED 121
Loss of Spiritual Support 121
Lack of Robust Discipleship 122
Devaluing the Role of Women 126
Low Literacy 128
Pride and the Unhealed Father Wound 130
A Weak Marriage and Busyness 132
Toxic Leaders 133

CONCLUSION 139

APPENDIX 1: FOR THE ROAD 147
Favorites from a Reformed Perspective 148
Other Favorites 150
Genesis 1 and Science: 151
Other Tough Topics 152
Favorite Commentaries 152

APPENDIX 2: How I Became a Christian Despite the Church Playlist 155

APPENDIX 3: Small Group Discussion Questions 157
Introduction 157
Chapter One: A River Ran Through It 158
Chapter Two: God Versus the Boulevard 158
Chapter Three: Shame, Distortions, and Abuse 159
Chapter Four: Breaking Free 159
Chapter Five: Healing Moves 160
Chapter Six: Sexual Staggers 160

    Chapter Seven: Learning to Love 161
    Chapter Eight: Finding God 162
    Chapter Nine: Why It Happened 162
    Conclusion 163

Acknowledgements **165**

About the Author **167**
    Dr. Greg Austen 167

INTRODUCTION

Spirituality wrongly understood or pursued is a major source of human misery and rebellion against God.[1]
—Dallas Willard

When Mary reached out on Facebook, I was hesitant to accept her friend request. Forty years ago, she, her younger sister, Grace, and I had all attended the same church called Berachah, and its accompanying school. Mary and Grace were two of Pastor and Mrs. Janson's sixteen children. Two of the eleven foster kids who regularly ate rejected, scratch-and-dent cans of cold, Campbell's split pea and pepper pot soup. Given a can opener and plastic spoons, they ate outside, while the Jansons' three biological and two adopted children fared better inside at the dining room table.

Treated like slaves, most of the foster boys slept in the basement or outside in sheds. Mary and the other foster girls slept on the porch floor. Showers were taken outside with no hot water. Since the fosters did the majority of the cleaning, laundry, and cooking, they missed a lot of school. They either didn't get a full day in or were shipped off early, before school, to work at the church.

Mary was also one of the kids who was beaten repeatedly, including at times on the soles of her feet or palms of her hands so the Division of Youth and Family Service workers wouldn't see the bruises. I only wish that was the extent of the cruelty and abuse children suffered at Berachah.

---

[1] Dallas Willard, *The Spirit of the Disciplines*. (San Francisco: Harper & Row) 1988, 81.

And yet, in what initially seemed like some weird form of Stockholm syndrome, when I accepted her friend request, she wanted to reminisce about Berachah via Messenger. She shared photos of a grade school class and a birthday party we had both attended. Truthfully, she probably just wanted to connect, to find a way to salvage something of her past. I felt bad, and although I accepted her request, thanked her for the pictures, and certainly wished her the best, I couldn't join her in any celebration of those years.

In researching this project, I've been forced to pore over pictures like the ones Mary sent, as well as other family memorabilia from "the Berachah years." As I do, I'm overcome with grief and anger. The church was supposed to help these people—to keep them safe, strengthen marriage and family, and provide trusted spiritual direction. But instead it misled, used, and abused them, and then a decade later left them on the side of the road, broken, and, in many cases, worse off than before they "found God."

Not surprisingly, most of the children I grew up with have little interest in God or the church. Many struggle with addictions and the idea of a good God, especially when so many bad things are done in his name. Some, like Mary, also have a hard time accepting God's love because of what happened, or because of what they've done since to escape what happened. Mary's sister, Grace, struggled for years in these same ways too, but not anymore. She died of an overdose in 2016.

Given the experiences my family, friends, and I suffered as a result of "following God," I'm often surprised that my own faith is still standing. Incredulously, I'm now a Presbyterian minister and leader in a national Christian ministry that champions human dignity and reminds our culture, including the #Metoo movement, that pre-natal men and women matter, too. But my relationship with the church is complicated. I love it because God loves it, Jesus died for it, and said the gates of hell would not prevail against it.[2] I want people to know that church experiences like Berachah weren't

---

[2] Matthew 16:18.

God, shouldn't be blamed on God, and were rather a rebellion *against* God.

But the church can be a mess and—worse—a real source of misery. I know. I've witnessed it. There are tons of hypocrites and even dangerous wolves in sheep's clothing. Lots of folks that are afraid of mainstream science and of learning from "secular" people. It often amazes me that those who read and study the least often have the strongest opinions about the questions that trouble us most. And then there are the emotionally unhealthy whack-jobs, charismaniacs, prudish "church ladies," and end-times crazies, because, as N.T. Wright has observed, with religion "there is always the danger of fanaticism, of a self-induced and self-promoting 'zeal'."[3]

Unique Take

Despite all this, I identify as a churchman. I have a unique, down-to-earth perspective, however, as I'm also a carpenter and the son of a land surveyor. Jesus was a carpenter and the Son of God. There's infinite space between these realities, yet that's the space I've inhabited most of my life. Carpentry is a humble, earthy trade that has kept me grounded. Being earthed in the real world is a good quality for pastor-theologians who reflect, speak, and write about heavenly concepts—that is, if they want to connect in a way that helps people. Life is messy and full of struggle. Rot and decay are all around. But being a skilled craftsman gives me the opportunity to beautify a certain space—to strengthen, support, renovate, renew, create, and build up. This is part of what's most satisfying about being a carpenter: you have something to show for your labor at the end of the day.

The work of a pastor-theologian is less tangible, but there is still great opportunity to assess and address rot and decay, repair foundations, and bring beauty, clarity, and strength to faith and life. Like the carpenter, the theologian also works with space—that vast,

---

[3] N.T. Wright, *Lent for Everyone: Mark, Year B* (Louisville: Westminster John Knox Press, 2012) 35.

infinite, eternal space between us finite humans and God. Theologians deal in the renovation of the heart and celebrate the God who initiates relationship and draws us near.

And that's the God I hope you come to know in a deeper way as I share my story of how I became a Christian despite the church—particularly one really destructive and harmful church called Berachah. If you're a skeptic or a seeker, or even if you don't believe in God, I hope you'll feel respected as you read this book. And I hope that what follows will challenge, surprise, and inspire you with love and meaning.

In recounting my experience, I've changed many names.[4] I have no wish to further hurt people who are still trying to move on with their lives. Some of the details, however—especially the crimes against children, are a matter of public record. In these instances, I've given source information in the appropriate footnotes. In retelling all, I've tried to be as accurate as possible.

Although I'm not a stand-up comic or late-night talk show host—the trusted purveyors of knowledge in our day, in what follows there are definitely lots of you've-gotta-be-kidding, truth-is-stranger-than-fiction stories. These are dovetailed together with lots of honest questions, research, and practical help. To provide minimal distraction and clutter, and yet still promote maximum engagement with the Bible, I've included most references in the footnotes.

Constructive Tone

Unlike many popular deconversion stories,[5] I've tried my best to avoid this kind of formula:

- "Step 1: Recount the Negatives of Your Fundamentalist

---

[4] I did not change the name of Berachah; however, that church no longer exists and should not be confused with any other church by that name.

[5] De-conversion stories are designed to reach Christians, not to reach non-Christians, and their purpose is to convince them that their outdated, naïve beliefs are no longer worthy of their assent. Bart Ehrman, Rob Bell, Peter Enns, and Jen Hatmaker are examples of authors who have written in this genre.

- Past
- Step 2: Position Yourself as the Offended Party Who Bravely Fought the Establishment
- Step 3: Portray Your Opponents as Overly Dogmatic While You Are Just a Seeker
- Step 4: Insist Your New Theology Is Driven by the Bible and Is Not a Rejection of It
- Step 5: Attack the Character of Your Old Group and Uplift the Character of Your New Group"[6]

My goal is rather to handle scripture responsibly, maintain a constructive tone, own my stuff, and avoid villainizing everybody else but me.

At the same time, *like* many deconversion stories, shame, abuse, and especially distorted views of sex are major themes. If you or someone you love has struggled or suffered in these areas, you'll find hope and clarity in the coming pages.

As you'll see, although I do want to take an axe to repression, I have no interest, as many are now doing, in radically "redefining the stale and oppressive sexual ethic the church has taught for so long."[7] I'm rather with those who still believe that "chastity and celibacy are good and sex is *necessarily* covenantal."[8]

Here are some of the other topics I explore in the coming chapters:

- What's a Christian response to culture that promotes full engagement with life, as well as full enjoyment of the goodness of creation? What is one that preserves

---

[6] These steps are detailed and taken from https://www.thegospelcoalition.org/article/jen-hatmaker-power-deconversion-stories/

[7] Nadia Bolz-Weber, *Shameless* (New York: Convergent, 2019), 198.

[8] Tish Harrison Warren, "The Church Made Vagina Sculptures Long Before Nadia Bolz-Weber," Christianity Today, Posted February 26, 2019. Anglican priest Tish Harrison Warren explains what she means by "covenantal": "When we have sex, our bodies are enacting a promise—two are becoming one flesh. That mysterious conjoining and fusing is a physical embodiment of the covenant of marriage. It's set up so that the person you sleep with is the one you do your taxes with and celebrate anniversaries with and struggle through long, dark years with and fight over the thermostat with, till death do us part."

appropriate caution but still encourages joy, courage, fun, and openness to others who think differently?
- What is a perversion of holy sexual desire and what is just religious baggage?
- How do we heal from the ugliest things that have been done to us or those we care about? We can repent of sin but what do we do with shame?
- How do we know if we've forgiven someone? And, if we forgive, do we have to reconcile?
- How do we safeguard our family from toxic leaders, bad-news churches, and abuse?
- How do we know when the Bible should be taken literally and when it shouldn't? How do we retain a rigorous use of our brain and handle such a dangerous book correctly?

Although this book is a roadmap for healing and growth for all, it's especially written for those who've been hurt or turned off by religion. In pulling together themes, I've utilized insights and illustrations from individuals, thinkers and artists as diverse as Maya Angelou and Madonna, the Apostle Paul and Paul Simon, Elton John and Tolstoy, as well as movies from *Star Wars* to *David Copperfield*.

The first chapter details my early faith and family, sets the stage, and gives context for the remainder of the story. The next three chapters are focused on the center of the "bad religion" story—what happened (chapters 2-3), as well as how I broke free (chapter 4). The middle three chapters laser in on the healing process, including those areas in which I still walk with a limp (chapter 5), have struggled the most (chapter 6), as well as the most important thing I'm still learning (chapter 7). And the final two chapters concentrate on my intellectual journey and "reasons of the heart:"[9] why I still believe (chapter 8), analyses of why this toxic church experience happened to my family—including seven key lessons (chapter 9), and the resources that have helped me the most to

---

[9] Blaise Pascal famously said, "the heart has its reasons of which reason knows nothing."

address questions, handle the bible correctly, and grow as a Christian (appendix 1). Also, for those interested, I've included a really cool playlist (appendix 2) and questions for discussing this book in a small group (appendix 3).

Finally, in thinking about the quote with which I began this introduction, and in assessing all that follows, it's helpful to both define and show the subtle difference between spirituality and religion. *Spirituality* is caring for who you are on the inside and, from a distinctly Christian view, trusting Christ to help you change from the inside out and learn to love. *Religion* is the system of beliefs, the external structure—like a church community or a holy book like the Bible—that helps you pursue spirituality. Religion can be true[10] or false. Something that brings life, heals, and builds up or something that kills, maims, and destroys.

I pray that this story of spirituality wrongly understood and pursued will give you—and all those you love—a trusted path to the former and discernment to avoid the latter.

---

[10] James 1:27.

CHAPTER ONE: A RIVER RAN THROUGH IT

I remember your genuine faith, for you share the faith that first filled your grandmother Lois and your mother, Eunice. And I know that same faith continues strong in you.
—the Apostle Paul (2 Timothy 1:5, NLT)

My grandmother wasn't named Lois, but my mom was and she's associated with my earliest spiritual memory.

I was three and at Bushkill Falls, "The 'Niagara of Pennsylvania,' and among the Keystone State's most famous scenic attractions. This unique series of eight waterfalls, nestled deep in the wooded Pocono Mountains, is accessible through an excellent network of hiking trails and bridges…."[1]

It's a beautiful place that fills your senses with the smell of pines, fabulous views of the falls and the surrounding forest, and the constant and peaceful roar of rushing water.

Signs at the park warn visitors not to stray from the trail or jump the solid wood fences that block access to the falls. The reason? People slip, fall, and there have been several deaths over the years. For example, in 1992, a 13-year-old ran ahead of his camp leader, slipped and tumbled down an icy, 100-foot bank, plunging into the frigid white torrent where he soon drowned.[2] Again, in

---

[1] https://www.visitbushkillfalls.com/
[2] http://articles.mcall.com/1992-02-03/news/2843774_1_pine-trees-water-robert-hicks

2011, another teenager walked off the marked trail and, climbing across a steep embankment, lost his footing and fell into the falls. He was pronounced dead at the scene.[3]

My mom was concerned. She had recently read in the newspaper of a child who had fallen to his death at Bushkill and now here, with my father, six-month-old sister, and me, she understood why. Back then, access to the falls in some sections was blocked only by ropes, not sturdy fences. An unprotected and ornery three-year-old like me could easily go over the side, especially if they tripped while running.

As we entered the park and approached the falls, parents were instructed by park rangers to hold on tightly to their children and keep them close. Taking me aside, my mom looked straight in my eyes and told me about the boy who had fallen to his death. She told me candidly that if I didn't listen and hold on tightly, I might fall and get killed. That was all the warning I needed. I clung fast to my mother's right hand as she cradled my sister against her with her other arm.

My mother's hand was there. I could trust it and, as long as I held it, I was safe. As an adult, I now know that was no small thing.

Trust. It's the foundation of all relationships: spouses, parents and children, friends, business partners—even our relationship with God. As many believe, part of the divine design is that children learn about trust ideally *first* from good parents. These experiences are far more spiritually formative than any Sunday School class. As Erik Erikson[4] pointed out in his 8 Stages of Psychosocial Development, trust versus mistrust is the first psychological conflict that must be successfully overcome for a child to develop into a healthy, well-adjusted adult:

> Unresponsive caregivers who do not meet their baby's needs can engender feelings of anxiety, fear, and mistrust; their baby may see the world as unpredictable. If infants are treated

---

[3]http://www.poconorecord.com/apps/pbcs.dll/article?AID=/20110813/NEWS/110819865/-1/news
[4] 1902–1994.

cruelly or their needs are not met appropriately, they will likely grow up with a sense of mistrust for people in the world.[5]

Geographic Roots

I was raised by two parents who loved me and grew up in Bridgeton, New Jersey, along the Cohansey River. This muddy, stagnant, and polluted river was quite the contrast to the moving, pristine tributaries of Montana seen in the movie, *A River Runs Through It.*[6] Besides the beautiful cinematography, I've always been enamored at how the movie captures something of the beauty and mystery of life: the quiet strength of familial love, our profound need for grace, and our lack of control over others' choices. Thankfully, the river that runs through all of our stories is ultimately connected to the mercy that flows from God's throne: "There is a river whose streams make glad the city of God…."[7] Only a "refuge and strength" river like that can sustain us through life's adversity and changes—even changes that occur in the areas we grow up in.

Cumberland County's once rich heritage and economy were developed around food, textile, and glass industries, as well as river and maritime trades. But years of decline have made it a convenient place for prisons, and a place of spiritual, educational, and cultural illiteracy.

Lots of peach orchards, corn fields, pine trees, sandy soil, and the best-tasting strawberries and tomatoes coexist alongside illiteracy, racism, addictions, and broken homes. True grit and simplicity meet a lack of desire to read, grow, or learn from others outside their narrow, independent world. Beaches and boardwalks but lots of poverty. Small towns but lots of small-mindedness.

My family's love aside, it was these negative things—combined with "bad religion" and my parents' later divorce—that fueled an unconscious decision to spend twenty years of my life despising my

---

[5] https://courses.lumenlearning.com/teachereducationx92x1/chapter/eriksons-stages-of-psychosocial-development/
[6] Directed by Robert Redford, this movie is based on the 1976 semi-autobiographical novella by Norman Maclean.
[7] Psalm 46:4a, ESV.

roots. This mentality even affected how I carried my identity as a carpenter in adulthood. Carpentry is a blue-collar trade and I wanted to be a white-collar guy that could have gone to Princeton. As an adult, I didn't like the fact that my undergraduate education was a hodge-podge of lesser known schools, one of which was a community college. Consequently, I spent most of my twenties and thirties carrying and trying to hide a cynicism I didn't fully understand.

The Poor Parson and His Wife

Although this bitterness was deep-seated and real, it was overblown as I was given excellent guidance in my formative years by my parents, an aunt and uncle, and both sets of grandparents—especially on my mom's side. In fact, my mother's father, Ralph Seaman, was a Lutheran minister with the Evangelical Lutheran Church and southern New Jersey was just one of the places he pastored.

Like St. Francis of Assisi, he loved animals, especially dogs. Along with Werther's caramels he later carried with him for his grandkids, he always had treats for the pets. And, like one of his other luminaries, Luther, he related well to the common man and had a clever, earthy sense of humor. His favorite show was *Everybody Loves Raymond* and he named his black dachshund, "Poopsie" because of her frequent accidents while being housebroken. Or, to change things up, he would call her "Piddles".

In many ways, my grandfather was the Poor Parson of Chaucer's *Canterbury Tales*. The Poor Parson didn't have much money, but he was rich in holy thoughts and deeds. He was the antitype to the other three central religious figures in the story: the Monk, the Friar, and the Pardoner. The Monk, instead of being devoted to work and prayer like other Benedictine monks, was devoted rather to hunting and eating. The Friar, unlike other good friars, was unscrupulous and accepted bribes. And the Pardoner was a charlatan, "officially" forgiving people's sins for a price.

Unlike these characters or the pastor you'll meet in the next chapter, my grandfather was the real deal. Yes, he struggled with depression and was broken and flawed like the rest of us; however, he was the opposite of the televangelists Bono mocks in "Bullet in the Blue Sky," or Neil Diamond in "Brother Love's Travlin' Salvation Show," or Phil Collins in "Jesus, He Knows Me."

His wife, my grandmother, was Mary and there was definitely something about her. She always had a smile and loved to laugh. Of German descent and with a twinkle in her eye, she looked a lot like a plump Ingrid Bergman. And there were aspects of her speech, heart, and manner that reminded me of Winnie the Pooh. She left our family an uncommon legacy of strength, unselfishness, and unconditional love.

Grandma Mary watched me frequently. I have memories of her reading stories like *Angus and the Ducks* and poems like "Wynken, Blynken, and Nod." She took me to pick blueberries, to feed the ducks, and to swim at the YMCA. In the late sixties and early seventies, it was a less dangerous world in small town Millville. For instance, at five and accompanied solely by my next-door neighbor who was only a few years older than me, my grandma gave me some change to walk to the 7-Eleven to get penny candy. My favorites were the Pixie Stix, Smarties, Squirrels, and Mary Janes.

I remember being seven and taking a bicycle ride with her. Not paying attention, I turned in front of my grandmother, causing her to brake to protect me. In horror, I watched as she flew forward over the handlebars, landing on her face and hands. Thankfully, her injuries weren't severe, but she did skin-up her hands and bruise herself pretty badly. I felt terrible. She scolded me but only gently. Looking back, I know she was in a lot of pain, but her attention quickly turned to comforting me.

Mary also passed on a great appreciation and respect for nature. On my mom's side, I was the only grandson surrounded by three granddaughters—my sister and my aunt Linda's two children. Every year, Mary would buy us subscriptions, as was appropriate for our age, to either *Cricket* magazine, *Ranger Rick*, the *Big Back Yard*, or *National Wildlife*. She was concerned about the environment before it was in vogue to do so. As Maya Angelou would later write, while she knew herself as a creation of God, she also saw herself as obligated "to realize and remember that everyone else and everything else are God's creation."[8] Mary loved the outdoors, a passion reflected in her favorite hymn, "Morning Has Broken."

Although my grandparents had little money, my Grandma enjoyed traveling and seeing new places. When my grandfather moved several times to new parishes, my grandmother never minded. She enjoyed new cultural experiences and was involved in her community. Consistent with this, she was open and always learning. Reasonable rather than repressive, she didn't want her children or grandchildren to be inappropriately sheltered.

Formative Views of Sexuality

It's a major theme in my story—one I'll detail more in later chapters, but one of the things I've had the most trouble extricating myself from is a distorted view of sex. For a good part of my life, there've been no Houdini moves I've been able to learn to completely escape the suppressive straight-jacket "gifted" me, primarily from the church of my adolescence. Looking back, even in the area of sexuality and a positive body image, my grandmother modeled a healthiness I've had to grow back into. Two memories stand out.

The first is from 1970 on one of our regular trips to the YMCA. I was four and with her in the women's locker room getting dressed. A middle-aged woman was standing in front of a sink and mirror after finishing her swim. She reached down, crossed her arms and pulled the top of her bathing suit up over her head revealing her breasts. I stood there staring. Eventually she and my grandmother noticed. The lady by the mirror just smiled kindly and my grandmother, embarrassed, quickly took me by the hand and pulled me over into another area. There was no scolding or shame, just a parental tug to avoid embarrassment. Being raised in a very modest family, this is my first memory of seeing a woman's breasts.

---

[8] Maya Angelou, *Wouldn't Take Nothing for My Journey Now* (New York: Bantam, 1994), 34.

The second memory is from 1973 during one of our trips to see my grandparents while my grandfather was pastoring in North Arlington, New Jersey, three hours from where I was born in Millville. My grandmother took me to see *The Three Musketeers*. It was rated PG and was a blend of action-adventure and comedy. But, being the 70's, it was a little bawdy. There's one scene where a sedan chair[9] is going by. Raquel Welch, who plays a clumsy version of Constance, in attempting to hide from her captors, jumps up and flattens herself against the windowed-side of the carriage. Arms stretched over her head and holding precariously on to the roof, the gentleman inside sees her cleavage pressed perfectly—albeit, accidentally—in front of the small framed opening. Eyes widening, he smiles at this unexpected good fortune.

My grandmother, while joining in the laughter at the awkwardness of the moment, nonchalantly tried to put her hand over my seven-year-old eyes. Again, this is another formative memory—my first glimpse of attractive cleavage on the big screen, but it's not associated with shame or disgust.

I also find it interesting that, in line with "the faith that first filled your grandmother… and your mother…" theme this chapter began with, besides my grandmother's early formative influence related to sexuality,[10] it was my mom who had the courage to sit down and read me a book about the birds and the bees. The catalyst was my coming home from first grade with a note from my teacher after I was encouraged by a couple of classmates to say the F-word really loud several times.[11] My mom tells me that when she got into

---

[9] A sedan chair or litter is a small windowed cabin with a seat designed to carry one occupant. It is carried by two porters (or "chairman") in front and two in the back using wooden rails that pass through brackets on the sides of the chair.

[10] I am defining "sexuality" here as "recognition of or emphasis upon sexual matters."

[11] Some might question whether first grade is too young to have "the birds and the bees" talk. But as the ministry Axis notes: "The 'Sex Talk' is a much bigger conversation that must be communicated in 100 1-minute conversations, not just ONE 100-minute conversation." For more, see

the details of the drawings about sexual intercourse, I said, "Eww… if I have to do that to a girl when I grow up, I'm never getting married!" It is amazing how time can change your perspective on these things!

The Double Helix of Faith and Family—Why it Matters

Faith and family, or the lack thereof—are powerful formative forces for all of us. Family, however, plays a far greater role in the development of our faith and overall view of the world—including our sexuality—than is commonly understood. Before diving into the details of my story, I'd like to take a deeper look at the larger context of the 2 Timothy passage that opens this chapter and introduce a concept called "the Double Helix of Faith and Family" developed by Mary Eberstadt, senior fellow at the Ethics and Public Policy Center. Eberstadt's concept, when viewed against the backdrop of the 2 Timothy passage, has huge implications for all of our stories—the ones we've inherited, as well as the ones we're now writing:

> I thank God whom I serve, as did my **ancestors**… as I remember you constantly in my prayers…. I am reminded of your sincere faith that dwelt first in your **grandmother** Lois and your **mother** Eunice and now, I am sure, dwells in you as well…. Follow the pattern of the **sound words** that you have heard from me, in the faith and love that are in Christ Jesus. By the Holy Spirit who dwells within us, **guard the good deposit** entrusted to you… May the Lord grant mercy to the **household** of Onesiphorus, for he often refreshed me…. (select verses from 2 Tim. 1:3-16, ESV; words in bold, mine).

Paul notes that both he (*"my* ancestors") and Timothy (*"your*

---

https://axis.org/product/membership-product-for-the-sex-talk/) Certainly, all conversations about sexuality should be addressed in developmentally appropriate stages and gradually over time. Here's the best series I've found to do that with younger children and adolescents: *God's Design for Sex* series, 4 Books from Navpress.

grandmother... *your* mother") have a heritage of faith." We also see this as well in v. 16 where it mentions "the household of Onesiphorus."

We all know that the role of parents and grandparents is vital. Parents are:
- Providers—related not just to financial provision but also providing emotional and physical presence, healthy meals, etc.
- Nurturers—connecting with your kids heart-to-heart
- Guides—passing on morals and values

In Paul's words above, there's a "good deposit" that *we* are supposed to guard (14). What is it? Verse 13 explains that this deposit is "sound [or healthy] words." "Sound words" are good teaching, and good teaching is an investment in your life and those God has called you to serve. Indeed, teaching is something parents and grandparents are doing all the time, either formally or informally. Think of the examples of my grandmother and mom above.

The research shows that the home—not the church—is the primary conduit for passing on the Christian faith. Sociologist Christian Smith analyzed data on who is really leaving the church and found "Parents are huge, absolutely huge, nearly a necessary condition" for a child to remain strong in their faith into young adulthood. He concluded, "Without question, the most important pastor a child will ever have in their life is a parent."[12]

Mary Eberstadt's *How the West Really Lost God* presents strong social science establishing that "More children equal more God. [And] More marriage equals more God."[13] Conversely, "detachment from those people most closely related to oneself"[14] equals less God.

She says faith and family are like a double helix; that is, similar

---

[12] https://www.thegospelcoalition.org/article/who-is-really-leaving-the-faith-and-why/
[13] Mary Eberstadt, *How the West Really Lost God* (West Conshohocken, PA: Templeton Press, 2013), 123.
[14] Ibid., 119.

to the structure of a DNA molecule. A DNA molecule consists of two strands that wind around each other like a twisted ladder. In the same way, she says, "the **family is not merely a *consequence* of religious belief but a *conduit* to it**."[15] What she means is that, when it comes to passing on a godly legacy, faith and family work together in an inseparable and integrated way like a double helix.

Let's discuss the two separate strands of Eberstadt's double helix:

- **Family is a *consequence* of faith** or the lack thereof. In other words, strong faith gives birth to strong families, or weak or no faith gives birth to fragile families. That's why many talk about "the breakdown of the family" in a nation that no longer trusts in God and has lost its moral compass. Less God leads to less marriage or the redefinition of marriage. What's more, the research shows that less marriage also leads to more poverty and more fragile homes.[16] And more fragile families result in fewer children growing up in healthy homes with a mom and a dad.

- **Family is also a *conduit* to faith**. As studies show, families form the primary channels for passing on faith, or the lack thereof. In the home, faith or its absence is both caught and taught. Again, Eberstadt's research shows that as a general rule "detachment from those people most closely related to oneself"[17] equals less God. This lens reminds us that even something simple like attending a special church service together as a family can strengthen faith.

Let's flesh out Eberstadt's double helix observations by thinking of a scenario where a son from a Christian home goes off to college, loses faith, becomes an atheist, and then decides to forgo

---

[15] Ibid., 101.
[16] See *Marriage and Caste in Society* by Kay Hymowitz for an excellent analysis of the research on this.
[17] Op. Cit., 119.

marriage and live with his girlfriend. On the one hand, the *family as consequence of faith* lens might seek to connect the dots between a gifted, unbelieving professor who dismantled the student's faith which then resulted in his viewing marriage as an antiquated and unnecessary concept. The *family as a conduit to faith* lens, on the other hand, might emphasize that the student's faith was weakened because he was separated geographically or emotionally from his biological family (or "household" to use Paul's words above) and this left him in a lonely, detached, and vulnerable state.

The takeaway from all of this is *not* that kids shouldn't go away or even to a "secular" school, but that faith *and family* are both primary drivers and equally consequential. We easily see and hear a lot about how loss of faith leads to a breakdown of the family. We hear little, however, of the power healthy family has to strengthen faith. Eberstadt's research suggests that when it comes to passing on a robust faith, proximity to family— the kind that includes plenty of heart-to-heart connection and time-spent—matters.

With that background, here's how Eberstadt's "family is a conduit to faith" played out in my family early on and how it was *one of the factors* that contributed to my mom's lack of spiritual support and vulnerability to bad religion.

The Double Helix Illustrated

There was a spiritual strength and stability that my mom's parents brought to our family just by their proximity. I was involved in special holiday programs at St. Paul's Evangelical Lutheran Church where my grandfather pastored for 15 years. Since our family would often share a meal together on Sundays, it was easy to go to church together. This enabled my mom to continue as a member at St. Paul's, which is also where she and my dad had been married. In fact, in those early days, even my agnostic dad would sometimes attend. That all stopped, however, when I was six and my grandfather accepted a call to a new church in North Arlington, New Jersey. He did so for good reasons but the loss of my mom's parents was sorely felt. As Eberstadt's research shows: "detachment from those people most closely related to oneself" equals less God. In our case, it's not like they took God with them out of the area, but we definitely lost a healthy spiritual influence.

As my mom recalls, when "they left, I lost, not only my mom and dad but also my whole church family—fifteen years of spiritual community. At St. Paul's, I had lots of spiritual moms and dads and now I was at a loss." Added to this, my grandfather—desiring to avoid any potential factions resulting from those that might not follow the new minister due to loyalty to the previous pastor, suggested that, when he and my grandmother left, my mom leave too.

As unnecessary and misplaced as this caution was, it left my twenty-seven-year-old mom largely alone geographically in her desire and struggle to retain church as a priority. A Lutheran "Preacher's Kid" at heart, she began attending Christ Lutheran ten minutes away in Bridgeton. Although fuzzy, I have positive memories of the pastor there who I'll call Pastor K.

During communion at Christ Lutheran, children were welcomed up front, although they could not partake of the bread and wine. Everyone would go up single file, children with their parents, and kneel at the altar where Pastor K stood. Pastor K was kind and made me feel safe. When it came my turn to see Pastor K, he would put his hand on my head and say some nice things about blessing and then give the adults in line a funny-looking white wafer and drink.

My mom came to have a slightly different take on Pastor K. Although she liked him as a person, he *didn't* make her feel safe and began to seek out her company more and more. She also later told me that Pastor K struggled with alcoholism and was eventually set up by a few of his parishioners. They encouraged him to drink too much in what he thought was a safe setting and then used his intoxicated state as evidence to oust him. All this—her discomfort with his advances and the unchristian way certain prominent members took advantage of his addiction—made her decide to leave.

Still feeling lost without her parents nearby yet knowing she needed to go somewhere, she called my dad's oldest sister to see if she could go with her. At my aunt's church, First Methodist, they were studying *The Late Great Planet Earth* by Hal Lindsey.[18] My mom recalls hating it because it seemed like science fiction and didn't fit with the rest of what she knew about the Bible. The experience at First Methodist and before that at Christ Lutheran following my grandparents move represents an unsettled, and transitional time in my family's faith journey.

The larger point in all of this, however, is to illustrate the "family is a conduit to faith" side of Eberstadt's Double Helix research and, especially, this primary insight related to the verse we began this chapter with: **It's harder to make investments in a way that "faith continues strong" when your "genuine faith" is rarely seen or lives far away.**[19] Although there are many legitimate reasons and circumstances that cause families to move away from each other, geographic distance *does* affect influence and involvement. Again, the Double Helix of faith and family is real and is one of the factors—there are others I'll detail later—that contributed to my mom's lack of spiritual support and vulnerability to the cult-like place where we ended up next.

---

[18] Apart from the Bible, *The Late, Great Planet Earth* by Hal Lindsey was the most popular work of "non-fiction" in the English language in the 1970's. It later became a film and represents a literal, dispensational end times perspective. Dispensational theology emphasizes the distinct separation of Israel from the church and a pre-tribulational, secret Rapture.

[19] For important caveats and further analysis of this research, see: https://www.carpentertheologian.com/the-double-helix-of-faith-and-family-part-3-of-4-important-caveats/

CHAPTER TWO: GOD VERSUS THE BOULEVARD

Jesus freaks out on the street handing tickets out for God.
—Elton John, *Tiny Dancer*

When a Lutheran preacher's kid and an unchurched agnostic begin to raise kids together, there's bound to be tension. In many ways, it's a mini-household version of the culture wars—"God" versus "the boulevard" if you will. My first memory of this conflict was when I was five.

It was a Sunday morning and I was in the basement helping my dad build a wooden chest. My mom called down to tell me to get ready for church. I started to cry because I wanted to stay with my dad which, then, brought my mom to tears because she wanted me to go with her. Apparently, there was a growing conflict between my parents regarding church because my dad lit into me and spanked me—something he rarely did—for making my mom cry. I wondered why I was so severely disciplined. I just wanted to be with my dad.

And for good reason. My dad was an interesting, creative, albeit, wounded soul, and it was hard to get his attention. He loved magazines like *Popular Science* and *Popular Mechanics* and, like MacGyver, he could make amazing things out of few or discarded materials. Ingenuity was his specialty. When I was in second and third grade, he helped me win first place in the school's science fair. We made a water drop microscope one year, and a working telegraph the other.

In those years, he had a "wild at heart" side to him and, in many ways, he was a man's man. As a boy, he loved to swim, fish, and camp. As a young adult, he became proficient on the trampoline and as a gymnast, scuba diver, and canoeist. In fact, in his early thirties, in true *Deliverance* fashion, he almost lost his life running a wing-dam into white water with some of his buddies. Among other things, he taught me to fish, split wood, and work hard. He believed in doing things well and would often say, "It is easier to do something right the first time than to explain why you didn't." He was part of a generation where women were the primary nurturers and men were the providers.

Despite feeling at retirement as many do that he had worked too hard for too little for too long, he really was an involved, responsible, and committed father. I have many pleasant memories of my dad. The earliest, from ages five to eight, are watching TV with him, especially shows like *Mod Squad*, *UFO*, *Adam 12*, and *Emergency*. I remember being with him when Muhammad Ali won fight after fight, Richard Petty and Mario Andretti won race after race, Evel Knievel attempted his jump of the Snake River Canyon, and the gymnast Nadia Comaneci earned her perfect tens.

One of our biggest points of connection as I entered later adolescence was reading *The Hardy Boys* books together. I had read these and other books voraciously for years, thanks primarily to my mom's efforts. She used summer vacations, the library, and a little ice cream shop called Daniel's to instill a life-long love of reading in my sister and me. Each year, our out-of-school routine began with a weekly trip to the public library where we checked out several books of our choosing. If we read one book that week, we got a small ice cream cone, two earned a large, and three or more a banana split. I went for the banana split every week and I read a lot of books each summer. That simple incentive paid such rich dividends that, to this day, I would buy *you* an ice cream just to let me read!

I shared a couple of my favorite *Hardy Boys* books with my dad: *House on a Cliff*, *While the Clock Ticked*, and *The Shore Road Mystery*. He read them, thoroughly enjoyed the experience, and then joined me in these adventures.

Tickets and Scalps

When I was seven, a definite change took place in our household. It all started with neighbors handing tickets out for God. Of course, they called the tickets "tracts"[1] and we learned later that the act of handing them out was called evangelism or "soul-winning." The church these neighbors went to had big red buses painted with the tagline "The church that's alive with the people with a heart." This church was called Berachah, a funky Hebrew word that was supposed to mean "blessing." Nothing could have been further from the truth.

Berachah's buses were sent out into the communities to bring in kids, but the greater strategy was to use the kids to get to the parents. In time, one of my neighborhood buddies invited me to go. I had a good experience, and asked my mom if we could start going to this church. This pleased her, as she was weary of the tension and growing battle of getting me to church. She began to attend, and soon responded to one of their weekly altar calls, making a profession of faith. She recalls, "There was something I had been searching for that I hadn't found in the Lutheran church. At Berachah they believed in something, and they preached from the Bible, not just their interpretations of the Bible. It felt real. So I stayed."

As my mom settled into a new church "family," they began to send "soul-winners" to see my dad with more tickets from God. One of them, written by Pastor Janson, was called "The Agnostic Who Dared to Search." My dad, at first sparring with the erstwhile church-goers, eventually made a profession of faith too, and started attending this fundamentalist Baptist church called Berachah.

It was a busy, programmatic culture with something going on almost every night. I remember they had an acronym for JOY:

---

[1] A tract is Christian in-house language for a pamphlet on why you need Jesus.

- J—Jesus first
- O—others second
- Y—yourself last

Interestingly, the church viewed itself and all its programs as part of the "J—Jesus first." The "Y—yourself last" part was interpreted in a way that eliminated healthy boundaries, personal preferences, and individual expression. They justified this destruction of individualism by preying upon people's fears and any emotional or psychological unhealthiness. By setting themselves up as the only true, trustworthy representatives of God. They wanted clones—the kind that don't think deeply or question—to do "God's kingdom work," defined narrowly as the church's program and whatever else the pastor and his wife wanted. There was little time to mow your lawn, enjoy hobbies, vacation, or even be a good neighbor because it was more important to "win souls." After all, people were dying and going to hell, and, if you didn't warn them, their blood would be on your hands. Ignoring context and the limited application of the passage to the prophet Ezekiel's unusual role toward Israel specifically,[2] they forced us to memorize Ezekiel 3:18 and used it like a gun to our heads:

> When I say unto the wicked, Thou shalt surely die; and thou givest him not warning, nor speakest to warn the wicked from his wicked way, to save his life; the same wicked *man* shall die in his iniquity; but his blood will I require at thine hand.[3]

The salvation of the world was squarely in your hands, not God's, ignoring one of the central tenets of biblical Christianity:

---

[2] Again, Ezekiel's role is unique and should not be universally applied to all scenarios—especially with gun-to-your-head urgency. This is because: 1) It is unusual in that "God is both the one who appoints the protective watchman and the one against whom the watchman must be protected." 2) It is curious in that although four possible responses to Ezekiel's warning are considered, repentance is not one of them. This is "possibly an indication that Ezekiel did not really expect this case to occur." If it is universally applied, it "underlines the importance of the prophet's persistence in his task, even though he sees no apparent results." See *Harper Bible Commentary* (San Francisco: HarperCollins, 1988), 663-664.

[3] KJV.

"Salvation belongs to the LORD."[4]

The Ezekiel verse was quoted regularly to motivate members with fear and guilt. It created a sense of urgency where you could never relax. The person in the checkout line, for example, might go to hell if you didn't preach to them or give them a tract. God wasn't someone to have a relationship with or be enjoyed. He was the all-knowing, all-seeing evangelism task master with a whip who was only pleased when you performed well. Like our authoritarian pastor, Berachah's version of God wanted church initiatives—especially "soul-winning"—to be at the center of your life and the primary way you spent your time.

As a new Christian, my dad bought into all this hook, line, and sinker and began passing this urgency on to me. This is an excerpt from a letter he wrote me on Christmas day, 1976, just before I turned eleven:

> Dear Greg, I have some definite goals for your life... I want you to be completely dedicated to worthy Christian service... Be concerned about the lost. It's easy to sit back and enjoy your own salvation—but remember always—that you found out about Jesus only because somebody else was very concerned about you. Be a soul-winner. Be an on-fire Christian always trying to get the gospel to the lost. Make a kind of game of it. See how many souls in your lifetime you can really snatch away from Satan. Will it be 10? 50? 500? 10,000? It's up to you!

This get-a-scalp-on-your-belt-for-Jesus culture that Berachah hawked even added a fun, game-like spin to some of their best tickets from God: gripping tracts by the late Jack Chick that included *Crusader* comic books. These were attention-getting, sometimes graphic stories about two buff guys—one white and one black, God's two-man Mod Squad—who knew Bruce Lee moves and were off to save the world à la Chick's view of reality. Yes, these stories attempted to present the gospel clearly with vivid depictions of the death, burial, and resurrection of Christ but they reflected a

---

[4] Jonah 2:9b, ESV; Revelation 7:10.

myopic, shallow Christianity steeped in Arminian[5] and Dispensational[6] theology.

Sunday morning messages were always some variation on "the old, old [gospel] story" designed to get as many people to walk the aisle as possible. Although often laced with interesting stories, Pastor Janson's sermons were always guilt-inducing, full of shouts, and emotional manipulation. I recall once, after twenty or so stanzas of "Just As I Am" where no one had yet walked the aisle to "recommit their life to Christ," one old church pillar named Russ went forward just so we could all go home!

Another common Berachah refrain attributed to C.T. Studd was "Only one life twill soon be past. Only what's done for Christ will last." Again, this narrow focus on what you did for Christ evangelistically added a panic, uneasiness, and intensity to all of life. Why have a well-manicured lawn or a nicely landscaped property? Why enjoy a movie or cultivate a hobby? Jesus is coming back and everything's going to burn up, anyway. Everything was about mission, outreach, multiplication, and reproduction. Yet as Lesslie Newbigin has wisely observed, "…there's a name for cells in the body that only reproduce and don't do anything else for the rest of the body: cancer."[7]

I've seen this cancer first-hand and have come to understand that soul-winning is not the ultimate goal of life or even the church. John Piper says it well and clarifies what *is* the ultimate goal of life:

> Missions is not the ultimate goal of the church. Worship is. Missions exist because worship doesn't. Worship is ultimate, not missions, because God is ultimate, not man. When this age is over, and countless millions of the redeemed fall on their faces before the throne of God, missions will be no more. It is

---

[5] Arminian theology stresses the role of human responsibility and effort in obtaining salvation from God.

[6] Dispensational theology tends to emphasize a rigid distinction between Israel and the church and a literal, plain-sense interpretation of the book of Revelation; that is, one that is not primarily dependent on its Old Testament background, literary genre, or first century culture.

[7] https://www.cardus.ca/comment/article/pastoral-care-as-public-theology-a-conversation-with-tim-keller/

a temporary necessity. But worship abides forever.[8]

Here's another healthy and historic expression of ultimate priorities from the *Westminster Shorter Catechism*: "The chief end of man is to glorify God and enjoy him forever."[9] I actually remember hearing this quoted at Berachah growing up, but it was the "glorify God" part that got emphasized, certainly not the "enjoy him." Further, even glorifying God was narrowly focused on their rules and questions like:

- Have you done your daily "devotions" or "quiet time"?
- How well do you perform "the eight musts for Christian living?" These were a list of eight rules they compiled and gave to each new Christian.
- Do you externally look like a Christian? For example, if you're a girl, you'd better not wear pants. Or, if you're a boy, you'd better not have your hair over your ears or parted in the middle (to have your hair parted in the middle in the 70's was thought to be a sign of rebellion!).

Returning to "God Versus the Boulevard"

Christians have a strange proclivity to fashion Jesus' teaching on the narrow way into a joyless pursuit that devalues creation and makes the world he created very small.

I've come to understand that to be a Christian doesn't mean that you have to see bad in everything that doesn't have a Bible verse on it or fit into the lyrics of "How Great Thou Art" or "God of Wonders". Now, don't get me wrong, I like both songs, but for some Christians their engagement with the outside world is very limited. Better make sure you're thinking about God constantly and, if you're with others—especially if they're not Christians, make sure you tell them often in your best Ned Flanders voice, "Diddly *dee*— God does amazing things, doesn't *he*?" I'm exaggerating a little, but

---

[8] John Piper, *Let the Nations Be Glad* (Grand Rapids: Baker, 1993) 11.
[9] I also like the Roman Catholic church's Baltimore Catechism on this question: Q: Why did God make you? A: God made me to know him, to love him, and to serve him in this world and to be happy with him forever in heaven."

the funniest caricatures are based on realities we've experienced or observed.

Of course, if you went to a Christian retreat center (in my area that was Sandy Cove or Word of Life), you got extra Christian street cred, especially if you spent at least fifty percent of your time listening to Christian speakers and singers. The message was loud and clear: Whatever you do, don't venture off into the city to see its manmade wonders. Cities are dangerous, as is culture. For example, if you went to an art museum, yes, you might see a picture of *The Last Supper*, but you might also see something that disrespects your faith or—worse yet—a nude. And God help you if you saw a woman's breast or a man's penis. I remember one time—and it's the only time I remember Berachah's school participating in an outside cultural event—we took a class trip to see *The Marriage of Figaro* by Mozart. Fifteen minutes into the opera, we ended up disrupting things—getting up and walking out, because one of the singers came out in a dress that showed too much cleavage. Again, better to stay away in your own little world. Keep away from the dangers. Go to that Christian retreat center or conference, instead. Or better yet, save your money and give it to the church. That way you'll also have more time and increase the probability that you'll save more souls.

More on Culture & the World

I don't want to diminish the real dangers of the world or culture. As Cat Stevens sang, "Oh, baby, baby, it's a wild world" and there is need to "take care." Think of all that's on the internet. The Bible *does* teach that Christians are to keep themselves from being squeezed into the world's mold[10] and part of true religion is "refusing to let the world corrupt you".[11]

The problem at Berachah, however, was that all *culture* was bunched together with the evil *world* and then jettisoned to a place where "true" Christians had no business going. The boulevard was

---

[10] Romans 12:2.
[11] James 1:27, NLT.

all bad and you'd better stay away from it. Exceptions were made for certain classic films or shows like *Little House on the Prairie,* but it wasn't safe to venture much past these. Berachah and other churches like them practiced what Jamie Smith calls the "pietism of withdrawal;" that is, the abstention from culture itself. I have come to learn that this abstention, under the guise of keeping people from sin, actually cheapens human existence and is in violation of God's command to "fill" the world and "have dominion" (Gen. 1:26-28).[12] It further chains good people from deeper worship, as they never learn to enjoy God or bask in His goodness expressed in creation. Finally, it's a clear violation of Paul's teaching in Colossians 2:20-23, and a form of the heresy Gnosticism where the body is viewed as evil:

> "Since you died with Christ to the elemental spiritual forces of this world, why, as though you still belonged to the world, do you submit to its rules: "Do not handle! Do not taste! Do not touch!"? These rules, which have to do with things that are all destined to perish with use, are based on merely human commands and teachings. Such regulations indeed have an appearance of wisdom, with their self-imposed worship, their false humility and their harsh treatment of the body, but they lack any value in restraining sensual indulgence."

Jamie Smith in his book *Desiring the Kingdom*, gives clarity to the different ways the Bible uses *world*:

> "Clearly the meaning of *world* in Scripture is not univocal [that is, it doesn't just have one meaning]; it can refer to various phenomena and realities. I suggest that the most helpful distinction to make when encountering reference to 'the world' is an earlier distinction we made between 'structure' and

---

[12] This "filling" or "dominion" are often called "culture-making." Again, Jamie Smith gives this helpful definition: "Culture-making– unfolding the latent possibilities that have been folded into creation– is a vocation given to us as image bearers of God. Just as the Fall means not that we stop desiring but rather that our desires become disordered, so too sin does not mean that we stop being culture makers; rather, it means that we do this poorly, sinfully, unjustly." (*Desiring the Kingdom*, 178.)

'direction.' With that distinction in hand, we can suggest that, on the one hand, the Scriptures affirm the world as *structure* (as a given reality) is created by God and, as such, is fundamentally good. On the other hand, *world* is sometimes a sort of name given to human society that has taken the world (as structure) in the wrong *direction*. In that case, the world names fallen, broken systems, idolatrous configurations, the Garden of Eden remade as Babylon."[13] [14]

In recovering from soul-killing and life-diminishing churches like Berachah, one is left with a crucial question: How do individuals and Christian families live in the world or this culture without becoming part of it? Rick Warren, in *The Purpose Driven Church*, offers three ways a person can relate to culture:

- **Imitation:** Some people are not aware of how culture affects them or others. They become carbon copies of the culture around them. Culture, not Scripture, directs their moral compass.
- **Isolation:** Some people remove themselves from the culture to avoid "the pollution of the world."[15] There are certainly some merits to the age-appropriate protectionism inherent within this perspective, but there is little interest in engaging people or the culture.
- **Influence and Engagement:** This is what Jesus teaches His followers in Matthew 5:13–16: Let your light shine so that people will see your good works and glorify God. This is also consistent with the Bible's teaching of being "in the world but not of it."[16]

Consistent with the "influence and engagement" approach to culture above, Tim Keller notes that "our stance toward every human culture should be one of critical enjoyment and an

---

[13] James K. A. Smith, *Desiring the Kingdom* (Grand Rapids, MI: Baker, 2009) 188.
[14] For scriptures that affirm the world as *structure*, see John 1:10, 3:16, Acts 17:24. For scriptures that affirm the world as *direction*, see Rom. 12:2, James 1:27, 1 John 2:15, 5:19.
[15] James 1:27.
[16] John 15:19; John 17:14-16.

appropriate wariness."[17] He further remarks that "Paul does not simply dismiss a culture's aspirations; rather, he both affirms and confronts, revealing the inner contradictions in people's understanding. This is why it is so important to enter a culture before challenging it."[18] As Jeremiah 29:7 says, "…Seek the peace and prosperity of the city to which I have carried you into exile. Pray to the LORD for it, because if it prospers, you too will prosper." The culture around us fares better when we bless it with our influence and contribute our giftings to it, rather than avoiding it.

But that's not how Berachah schooled its followers. They taught the "isolation" option and then used plenty of fear and shame to manipulate, control, and make sure everyone—especially new believers—stayed in line.

Fun-suckers & Manipulators

I chewed a lot of gum that year. I was collecting trading cards for the movie that everyone was talking about—a movie that promised to be one of the greatest science fiction movies of all time, complete with amazing special effects—*Star Wars*.

My dad loved science fiction and was particularly excited about the movie. He was a big Trekkie and so was the draftsman that worked for him in the land-surveying business he had started two years prior. The movie event was going to be a family affair and we—my mom, my sister, and especially my dad and me—were counting down the days to the May 22, 1977 release.

As my deck continued to grow, I had been showing my *Star Wars* cards to my friends at the private Christian school Berachah had started. One day, a week or two before the movie's release, I mentioned my excitement to my friend, Fred, one of the pastor's three biological children. Oddly, he seemed a little concerned and less excited than I thought he should be.

Later I learned he went and told his parents of our family's

---

[17] Tim Keller, *City Church* (Grand Rapids: Zondervan, 2012), 109–110.
[18] Ibid., 124.

plans. My parents were then called, reprimanded, and that Sunday the pastor preached on the evil of going to the movies in such a way that my family was publicly humiliated. He said "we had a family this week that was planning to go see…" Although we weren't mentioned by name, everyone seemed to know who the pastor was talking about. In Berachah's culture, a seasoned member would never think of doing something like this or, if they did, they wouldn't be so foolish as to broadcast it and get caught. But my parents were the newbies—the baby Christians that like dumb sheep must be corralled and kept in line.

With the struggle of starting a fledgling new business, it was such a rare thing for us to do something this special. And this something special became a cultural and worldwide phenomenon. Most people remember the first time they saw *Star Wars*—not with the same vividness that they remember JFK's assassination, the Challenger explosion, or 9/11, but it's up there. Many families and individuals I've talked to over the years went and saw it several times. And we missed it. Why? Because of a stupid rule. Because of an abuse of authority. Yes, this is a first world "tragedy" and, in the grand scheme of eternity, it may not be a big deal, but the Church is famous for covering over destructive abuse. The truth is, in this instance, a local church—Berachah—stole a rare and significant moment of togetherness and fun from my parents and family. They robbed us of a simple, historic, and positive connection to global humanity. Good, clean, harmless, family fun that was none of their business. What's more, they did it in such a way as to shame and humiliate my mom and dad.

Stories like these still anger me because of the injustice, hypocrisy, and sheer idiocy some religious systems use to dominate, shame, and control their members. But to leaders of places like Berachah, it's all good because they need to use whatever is necessary to keep congregants from "the boulevard." This is the same ends-justifies-the-means thinking that is fine with using certain mediocre horror movies to scare children into heaven.

On May 10, 1975, I watched a movie at church called *The Burning Hell*, a film that is awarded one star and listed as horror/documentary on IMDb. It tried to scare people into heaven through literal, graphic depictions of what it's like to be in hell: worms eating at your face, screaming in eternal fire that never burns you up, and falling forever in total darkness.

The movie flashed back and forth between scenes from first century Israel and a modern story of a guy who rejects the gospel, has a motorcycle accident, and winds up in hell. In the biblical scenes, all Jesus' disciples had Southern accents and, even at nine, I thought that was strange.

During the invitation given after the movie, I began sobbing, not wanting God to send me to this terrible place. I went out and talked to a counselor who encouraged me to ask God to save me. I was eager to do so and asked God to forgive me and take me to heaven. I don't remember exactly what I said, but I do remember vividly, as I was leaving that night, looking up at the stars and being grateful and confident that God had heard my prayer and saved me.

For years, if someone asked me the specific date and details of my conversion experience—something more important in some Christian groups than others—I'd confidently say May 10, 1975 and tell them this story.

Today, I've come to see that what I viewed for years as a conversion story was actually religious trauma. In other words, what became etched in my memory was less because "I saw the light!," and more because that's what happens when you show horror movies to nine-year-olds. Yes, Proverbs does say "the fear of the LORD is the beginning of wisdom" (1:7), and I remain of the persuasion that, regardless of ones' view of hell,[19] the person who doesn't take God seriously is just not smart. But the ends (scaring children with horror movies) do not justify the means (coming to know God).

Unfortunately, all I've said up to this point is mild compared to what Berachah's bad religion brought next. Things grew more

---

[19] Years later, through further study, I came to understand and embrace the historic and metaphorical view of hell that is described and defended well in *Four Views on Hell* edited by William Crockett and published by Zondervan.

and more toxic in this distorted, authoritarian, increasingly shame-based, and—although we did not know it yet—secretly heinous church family.

CHAPTER THREE: SHAME, DISTORTIONS, AND ABUSE

When I think back on all the crap I learned in high school, it's a wonder I can even think at all.
—Paul Simon, "Kodachrome"

Influential and now scandalized mega-church pastor, Bill Hybels, is known for saying, "There's nothing like the local church when it's working right." The reverse is also true: There's nothing that can do as much damage as the church when it's not working right.

I spent 1973–1981, ages seven to sixteen, in a toxic environment called Berachah Bible Baptist—an independent church that morphed into something not far from a Kool-Aid-drinking cult.

It all began with the vision and aspirations of a new young pastor and his former Hollywood actress wife, Pastor and Mrs. Janson. The Jansons were a tall, attractive couple with a lot of charisma and energy. Shortly into their tenure, the church went through two splits. Most of the mature, discerning believers left, leaving the Jansons free to introduce a hyper-Christianity associated with the likes of Dr. Jack Hyles and the ultra-fundamentalist newspaper *The Sword of the Lord* founded by Dr. John R. Rice.[1]

Pastor Janson had a classic 70's door-to-door salesman look.

---

[1] Jack Hyles and John R. Rice, along with individuals like Jerry Falwell, were prominent leaders of the independent fundamentalist Baptist movement of the second half of the 20th century.

His black, horn-rimmed glasses rested on over-sized ears, and he had a slight gap between his two front teeth. Not surprisingly, his black hair was always neatly trimmed over his ears. He wore it parted on the side with a distinctive cowlick to give his rigid "fundy" persona a little flare. Most of the time he presented himself in a three-piece suit, and spoke with an air of authority which he carried into the pulpit. He fancied himself like his hero Charles Haddon Spurgeon, "The Prince of Preachers" from a by-gone era.

His wife, Mrs. Janson, was always fastidiously groomed and alternated wearing a wig or her natural jet black hair up in a French twist. She had a pretty, pale, gaunt face that exuded an, "I really care about you" attitude, especially to new believers. Many, in time, however, would come to learn just how skilled she was at using this charm against them. Mrs. Janson was one part Elizabeth Taylor and two very unpredictable parts Cruella Deville from the cartoon version of *101 Dalmatians*. She had an air of privilege and carried herself like a rich girl who had now condescended to work among the poor.

Together, the Jansons aspired to build "Berachah Christian City" on a ninety-acre piece of wooded land with running streams. And the majority of the work would be done on the backs of new believers like my parents. It would be a Christian community protected from an increasingly scary, godless world, with its own camp, school, place for seniors, and a large church at the center of it all.

My dad donated his time and did a topographical survey of the property to inform the vision and associated capital campaign. An artist's rendition of what the "city" might look like was painted on a huge signboard, divided into ninety sections, and placed at the front of the sanctuary. Congregants could then buy an acre, two, or more and get their name on the board. Besides the donated survey work, my dad worked many extra hours, sacrificing much, to pay for as many acres as possible. In the end, the land was never used for its intended purpose. Rather, twenty years later, the property was sold by a later generation to pay its bills. Not long after that, the church ceased to exist.

My parents gave cars to the needy, spent time with broken families, gave thousands of hours in counseling, visitation, Spanish ministry, running a bookstore, teaching, and more. My dad became, outwardly at least, the good "yes-man" deacon and my mom, his "submissive" wife.

In less than five years, the church grew from 200 to 900 people on a Sunday morning with three services. They had sixteen buses to pick up people from surrounding areas. They got an award for having the fastest growing Sunday School in New Jersey. The pastor even got on the Philadelphia news, made a big stink about the deteriorating morality in public schools, and subsequently started his own Christian school, where my sister and I were enrolled.

He and his wife, outward paragons of Christian virtue, took in thirteen foster children. The mayor gave them a key to the city. Outwardly it seemed like the perfect church. But inside things were rotting.

Eventually it surfaced that this pastor, our primary spiritual mentor, was a pedophile who abused several boys for years (more on that in a later chapter), and his wife a cruel, emotional and physical abuser. Both, in different ways, were deceitful manipulators behind the scenes. Most of the criminal acts played out in their personal mini-mansion or their home by the shore, but there were plenty of instances of shame and abuse that occurred at the church-school as well.

Although many from Berachah have scars greater than mine, the shame and abuse that affected me—the "crap I learned" in grade school and high school—are my story to tell. And, yes, it's definitely a wonder and a miracle of grace that "I can even think at all." As the late Emil Brunner said, barring God himself, "the most powerful of all spiritual forces is a man's view of himself, the way in which he understands his nature and his destiny, indeed it is the one force which determines all the others which influence human life."[2]

---

[2] Bruce Waltke, *Genesis, A Commentary* (Grand Rapids, MI: Zondervan, 2001), 67.

What follows, then, are those formative experiences of shame, distorted views of sex, and physical abuse that have had the greatest negative impact on my view of self.

Shame

When I was in fourth grade, there was a sixth-grade girl that I thought was stunning. Kate Murphy. What can I say? Everyone liked her. She was not only beautiful, she was kind. One day in morning devotions, it was my turn to lead and I read from *Our Daily Bread*. One of the words in the reading was "debris." I pronounced it as it looked, and the word came out like some strange combination of Debbie and humus. Kate came up to me afterwards, privately. Amused and with a twinkle in her eye, she told me that debris was French and was pronounced "debree." I'm sure my face turned all kinds of red, but she was so amazing and kind, I was happy to have even this interaction with her. Maybe just maybe, I thought, somehow she would be my girlfriend.

But I was a measly fourth-grader. What chances did I have?

Around this same time, I had done something wrong. I don't remember what it was, but Mrs. Janson had told me that I wasn't allowed to go anywhere in the building without someone going with me. That was fine. I was compliant and had no interest in getting in further trouble. One day, as we sat working away, facing the wall along a common desk that went around the perimeter of the room, separated by dividers into individual work spaces, Mrs. Janson came in hurriedly and interrupted our class. This, in and of itself, was not unusual. Her regular practice was to interrupt, regardless of what was going on, and get what she wanted.

This time she called me out of my seat and told me to hurry and go fill up her car, parked in front of the church's private gas pump, and then hurry back. The church had its own pump to easily fill the sixteen buses, as well as the Jansons' cars whenever they desired. Eager to please—especially Mrs. Janson—I took her keys and ran upstairs and outside to do what she asked. After finishing, I then quickly ran back downstairs to where she was still standing in the middle of the classroom. I looked at her, smiled, and handed her the keys.

Her face immediately clouded. Her eyes became fiery, as her lips curled into a snarl. "Didn't I tell you that you weren't supposed to go anywhere without supervision?" She said. "Yes, but—you told me to do this—" I stammered," I thought you knew…" Before I could finish, she grabbed me by the ear, yanked my head, and yelled, "You deceitful little sneak!" She then went on and on in front of the whole class about how horrible I was, as if I was the worst person the world had ever known. Everyone had turned around from their work stations and was watching. My heart sunk as, not ten feet from Mrs. Janson's hand and my ear, was Kate Murphy. I was so embarrassed. In Pain. Confused. I wanted to die.

Mrs. Janson's words and actions that day were very damaging. I had no idea at that time that she was a master manipulator. I only knew she made me feel like I was evil and a piece of shit. And then days or weeks later she would suddenly change, treating me like a spiritual young man with a good heart—the kind you would want your daughter to marry. Interacting with her and trying to predict her mood was psychologically traumatic.

Distorted Views of Sex

Mixed Bathing, Coors Girls, and Gothardism

I was ten years old and often a tag-a-long for various adults to do visitation for the church bus ministry. One lady I helped several times was my mom's friend, Jill Smith. One day (I was about ten-years-old), we stopped to see Mrs. Donnelly, the church secretary. She was an older, often mean-looking lady with bushy, black hair peppered with white. She had a four-foot high, above ground swimming pool and invited us to get cooled off. I gladly complied, as did Mrs. Smith and a young neighbor girl. We all played and had a great time. It was a lot of fun.

That was Saturday. The following Monday I was called into the school office by Mrs. Janson. She was again angry with me for my sneaky ways. Mrs. Donnelly had reported to her that I was mixed-bathing—a term that until that moment I had never heard. Mrs. Janson explained that the term meant swimming with someone of the opposite sex, something that in her mind was clearly off limits. I tried to explain that I didn't know, that Mrs. Donnelly had invited me to swim, and that the neighbor girl had just showed up. Mrs. Janson clearly doubted my sincerity and laid into me. The conclusion of this tongue-lashing was that I should have known to get out of the pool when the neighbor girl came over, and that I'd better remember this in the future.

This made no sense to me but was yet another way that shame was being reinforced, especially around my sexuality and inner motivations. In Mrs. Donnelly's mind, I had done this deliberately (I had not) and was a sneaky son-of-a-bitch. That didn't matter. I should have known. This experience taught me that boys and girls couldn't even swim and play together without it being something dirty.

Incidentally, Mrs. Donnelly's husband, Clarence, who was not a church-going man, hired me to mow their lawn one summer. He had several Playboy-type pictures in his shop, which I'm sure I found interesting. I didn't think much of it, though, because I knew he wasn't a Christian. When Mrs. Donnelly found out that he had these pictures out there, and that I had seen them and hadn't told her, she was angry. I explained honestly that I didn't think anything of it because I thought she knew. Again, these are the messages I heard: You're a "sneak," Christians are hyper-sensitive about sex and paranoid about what could go wrong, and if I was a better boy and Christian, I'd be a tattletale and watchdog like her.

Another one of Berachah's pharisees-in-training accosted my younger sister, Vicki, for telling a fellow first-grader how a girl "got raped" on the family-friendly show *Adam 12*. Although my sister was too young to understand the anatomical details, she was certainly old enough to know the term and that it was bad. Being overheard, however, set off the same kind of nonsensical chain of events as the mixed-bathing incident. Berachah's "holiness police" had once again done their job and called Vicki into Mrs. Janson's office and reamed her out. A sensitive child, my sister was not only as clueless and blindsided by this as I had been, but equally traumatized as well.

We lived an hour from Ocean City, New Jersey, but couldn't go to the beach. My aunt went regularly, and my extended family has many wonderful memories, but not our family. If Christians went to the beach, the logic went, boys might see a bikini-clad babe. And yet on the way to church every week, we passed huge billboards of bikini-clad babes promoting Coors beer. Go figure. I guess Berachah's logic was that they couldn't control the billboards, but they could keep a trip to the seashore from happening.

In later years, Berachah allowed its members to attend Institute in Basic Life Principles (IBLP) seminars where they learned more biblically distorted fundamentalism from IBLP's founder, Bill Gothard. Mr. Gothard's teaching includes a myriad of distortions, many of which misuse the original languages of the Bible and depend on the literal reading of a 500-year-old translation, the King James version (KJV). One example related to sexuality is his preference for the KJV reading of 1 Cor 7:1b: "It is good for a man not to touch a woman" over the NIV's more accurate rendering (the ESV is similar here) of this same reference: "It is good for a man not to have sexual relations with a woman." The translators involved with the NIV were more concerned to translate concept for concept, rather than word for word so that they got the meaning right. Mr. Gothard, however, was more interested in finding an easy proof text to keep boys and girls from "defrauding" one another and falling into pre-marital sex by not having any physical contact at all.[3] His approach ended up distorting the meaning of the text, and stealing natural, God-given freedom from friendships and dating relationships.[4]

---

[3] "Defrauding" is a KJV word he develops from 1 Thessalonians 4:6 and defines as "raising desires in another person that you cannot righteously fulfill." Combining this concept with the distorted rendering he gives 1 Corinthians 7:1b results in viewing any physical contact in the dating relationship as foreplay that will potentially lead to illicit sex.

[4] One friend commented: "This reminds me of Eve in the Garden adding to God's command by telling the serpent, 'We must not eat it or even touch it or we die.' Legalism always adds to God's Word and leads to death."

Regarding this same topic of sexual desire, Gothard promoted the memorization of and meditation on Romans 6–8 as a primary way to fight sins, including lust. Gothard gave personal testimony that as a single man, the result of making Romans 6:11 part of his life ("Reckon yourselves to be dead to sin") was that when an attractive girl walked by him he was literally "dead" to sexual desire and lust. Mr. Gothard's teaching here, however, is not fleeing lust; it is repression that borders on Gnosticism.[5] As Stan and Brenna Jones note, "Lust is more than noticing someone is attractive; it is deliberately using our minds to imagine sex that God says is wrong."[6] It occurs when we desire to have sex with someone who belongs to someone else.[7] Or it occurs when we objectify[8] another human created in the image of God, as in pornography.[9]

Although I'll say more about what a non-legalistic-yet-pure approach to Christian sexuality looks like later, suffice it to say now that it's taken me years to understand that *God* made most men to think attractive women in bathing suits look good and vice versa. This is a natural and normal thing. It's not perverted or predatory lust, although it can become so. Our sexuality is not a wetsuit we can extricate ourselves from. It is something that is part of the core of who we are. Like a flower,[10] it will age and fade, but it is

---

[5] Gnosticism is an early church heresy that claimed secret spiritual insight and knowledge, and taught that the body and the created material world were evil or inferior compared to the soul.

[6] Stan and Brenna Jones, *Facing the Facts: The Truth About Sex and You* (Colorado Springs, CO: Navpress, 1995), 111.

[7] Matthew 5:28.

[8] Or take pleasure in others objectifying themselves.

[9] Another friend who reviewed this project made the interesting observation that the "very act of choosing not to look at a woman out of principle is in and of itself objectification because it says 'I am incapable of looking in a nonsexual way.' It sexualizes the very act of a woman crossing your line of vision." She went on to say, "Having spent my fair share of time talking to men's foreheads and hairlines because they refused to look at me, this is a pretty testy topic for me."

[10] I am thinking here of Isaiah 40:8 rather than the "your virginity is a flower…once you lose your petals you lose your value" analogy that has done so much damage. For example, see Elizabeth Smart's testimony:

nevertheless beauty to be cherished, protected, surrendered to God, disciplined, and enjoyed. It is not to be loathed, despised, or repressed. In many ways, it is like a fine wine that matures over time as we figure things out and grow old with our spouses. God, the creator of our sexuality, has the right to define and steer us toward all that is good and pure. He does this, however, as a loving parent.

But that's not what I learned at Berachah.

Anatomically Correct Stick Figures

As one might expect, my mom—given her love for books—ended up running the church's Christian bookstore. The reason they had a bookstore, however, was less about literacy and more about controlling what their members read. There was already another excellent Christian bookstore downtown that was run by an American Baptist minister. But from Berachah's perspective, every other church and Christian organization in Bridgeton was sub-par and inadequate compared to them. Again, like it said on their buses, Berachah was "*The* church that's alive with the people with a heart."

The lengths they went to in order to control what people read or viewed were astounding. At one point, my dad, a gifted artist, was asked to do the illustrious job of using a black magic marker to color clothes onto anatomically correct stick figures from one of Francis Schaeffer's books. Some of the stick figures had circles for breasts and God forbid someone might lust over them! So, my dad dutifully colored them in with some kind of shirt or dress lest someone be offended or become obsessed with their genitals—or, worse yet, someone else's genitals.

Abuse

There was little accountability for how classroom time was spent in Berachah's school. Most of the teachers had no formal education or certification for what they were doing. They were

---

https://www.buzzfeednews.com/article/ellievhall/elizabeth-smart-obsession-with-purity-makes-rape-victims-fee.

"supervisors" or "monitors," self-appointed watchdogs for the pastor and his wife to do their bidding. Corporal punishment was carried out on a limited basis in the school. The arm of the church's authority, however, extended into the home, using parents as tools to carry out more severe physical punishment designed to break the child's spirit. Parents were not only told what to do, they were asked the next day if they did it.

After all, "The blueness of a wound cleanseth away evil: so do stripes the inward parts of the belly"[11] or as another translation puts this same verse even more candidly, "A severe beating can knock all of the evil out of you!" (CEV) Parents needed to just do what the Bible said. No need to think—just do it. It was like one of the popular sayings and songs of fundamentalists at the time: "God said it. I believe it. And that settles it for me."

Many good parents, I'm sure, felt in their gut that something was wrong with this kind of severity, but they were taught to hold God's Word, the Bible, as their highest authority and "lean not on… [their] own understanding."[12] They wanted good children who would go to heaven and not be squeezed into the world's mold. And so, they listened to their spiritual mentor who told them to take the Bible literally and do what it says: "Withhold not correction from the child: for if thou beatest him with the rod, he shall not die. Thou shalt beat him with the rod, and shalt deliver his soul from hell."[13]

This can be scary stuff in the hands of people of faith who blindly trust their leaders, prefer the King James Bible, and pride themselves in taking it literally. I personally am aware of children who were beaten over 100 times with one by three and one by two pieces of wood, boys being forced to pull down their pants and underwear for spankings at nine to fourteen years of age—an extremely abusive and shaming practice. As mentioned before, the Jansons often beat their foster children, targeting the palms of their

---

[11] Proverbs 20:30, KJV.
[12] Proverbs 3:5, KJV.
[13] Proverbs 23:13-14, KJV.

hands or bottoms of their feet so that DYFS would not pick up on any bruising in their routine inspections.

Most of the stories and extent of the physical and sexual abuse at Berachah are locked away in police and Division of Youth and Family Services (DYFS) reports, as they should be.

In the later years of the school, they started making use of what became known as the "bad room." This room was in a house across the parking lot from the church that had been purchased to lodge select staff that worked for the church or school. It also had a room run by a "warden," another new Christian young lady who had gotten pregnant out of wedlock, left her parents, and become "saved". Her job was to watch over and dole out punishment to disobedient students who were sent to the "bad room" to "serve time" for days, weeks, even months. These students did some of their schoolwork there, but would also periodically do jumping jacks and other exercises for long periods of time. These regimens were designed to break their spirits. This treatment was combined with instructions to "courageous" parents to severely spank—aka beat—specified kids who resisted or weren't sufficiently sweet and compliant. I remember several boys who ran away or attempted to during the time I was there. In fact, I seriously thought about it myself.

So how are we to interpret the passages of Scripture that seem to endorse physical or corporal punishment for harmful behavior?

Clearly Proverbs 23:13-14 affirms the place of corporal punishment in child rearing, even if "beating" is softened to some kind of swat or spanking.[14] Years later on the other side of Berachah, my wife and I made a limited use of spanking in raising our kids. We often looked for guidance to a ministry called *Focus on the Family* and a book, *Dare to Discipline*, by the organization's founder, phycologist Dr. James Dobson. Dobson taught that

---

[14] Scripture also affirms the ancient Near Eastern practice of stoning as an acceptable form of capital punishment but few, even those who ardently defend capital punishment as biblical, would insist that stoning *must* be the method used today. In the same way, practicing "biblically-sound" discipline need not mean we're beholden to one particular method of discipline like spanking.

spanking was best saved for serious offenses like lying, cheating, and deliberate or defiant acts of disobedience. To avoid abuse, his counsel was to use the age of your child to determine and limit the amount of times you spank them. For example, a two-year old gets two, and three-year old gets three, etc. His perspective was that, if used consistently in this way from an early age, spanking will not be needed in most cases beyond the ages of 6-8. Also, children—boys especially, being very susceptible to shame—should not be spanked past the ages of 8 or 9. Again, this is what we followed, and I'm convinced it at least helped us stay clear of abuse.

Today, after working for several years with incarcerated fathers who were often the victims of severe physical abuse and equated any discussion of discipline with beatings, I'm not convinced the use of corporal punishment is necessary or wise.[15] Further, "sixty countries, states and territories have adopted legislation that fully prohibits using corporal punishment against children at home...."[16] Although it's still legal in the homes of all U.S. states, there are an increasing number of high-profile organizations that believe it shouldn't be.[17] Here is the gentler approach to discipline that I have since learned.

1. Teach all that discipline comes from a Latin word "discipulus" meaning "to teach or to guide." Thus, the follower of a teacher is called a "disciple." Starting with this definition keeps the rich, broad, positive concept of discipline from being reduced to a synonym for punishment.
2. Discipline should be done by parents who first have a handle on their own emotions and anger. Otherwise,

---

[15] Again, I'm certainly not saying that discipline isn't essential or that a limited use of corporal punishment is morally wrong—only that I think the latter is unwise and unnecessary in our culture. I'm also trying to promote alternatives to spanking and "A New Way of Thinking About Discipline" that is promoted in *The Connected Child* by Karyn Purvis (New York: McGraw Hill, 2007).
[16] https://www.cnn.com/2018/03/12/health/spanking-laws-parenting-without-borders-intl/index.html
[17] http://www.gundersenhealth.org/ncptc/center-for-effective-discipline/resources/organizations-against-corporal-punishment/

discipline, in any form, will negatively impact children.
3. Learn to make use of the many excellent and appropriate methods of discipline beyond spanking (e.g. time-out, logical consequences, grounding, restitution, loss of privilege, etc.). Utilizing these alternatives to spanking avoids any risk or accusation of abuse.

Berachah's insistence on "beatings" as God's prescribed method of correction was criminal by today's standards and an epic fail at discipline. Today there are permanent scars in the memories of both victims and perpetrators. "Out damned spot" plays on in un-Shakespearean ways in the souls of children—now adults. It also plays on in a way that torments many of the adult perpetrators who are now wiser and free from the Svengali voices they once allowed to control them. Most church members were unaware of the severity of the physical abuse or any of the sexual abuse; however, many new believers and others close to the pastor and his wife were involved in repeated beatings of children. Tragically, the pastor's wife, Mrs. Janson, was front and center in most of this. She seemed to get off on the power and control while her husband hid in his ivory tower study using vulnerable children to get off in other ways. Throughout the years, a couple of the foster children had tried to beg for help, but they were quickly squelched, labeled pathological liars, and, in one case at least, put out of the home. Duped and devoted, like lemmings, all Berachites defended their "shepherd's" honor.

When I think back on all this horror, "crap" is such an inadequate word—I weep for all the victims and perpetrators. I resonate so much with this lyric by Randy Stonehill: "There are wounds time will not wash clean if we stood here forever in the rain." I have also been inspired by the strength, honesty, and courage of Rachael Joy Denhollander, the American lawyer and former gymnast who was the first woman to publicly accuse Larry Nassar, the former Michigan State University and USA Gymnastics doctor, of sexual assault. Her words from a 2018 interview with *Christianity Today* are a fitting conclusion to this chapter:

One of the areas where Christians don't do well is in

acknowledging the devastation of the wound. We can tend to gloss over the devastation of any kind of suffering but especially sexual assault, with Christian platitudes like *God works all things together for good* or *God is sovereign*. Those are very good and glorious biblical truths, but when they are misapplied in a way to dampen the horror of evil, they ultimately dampen the goodness of God. Goodness and darkness exist as opposites. If we pretend that the darkness isn't dark, it dampens the beauty of the light....

Yes. Church is one of the least safe places to acknowledge abuse because the way it is counseled is, more often than not, damaging to the victim. There is an abhorrent lack of knowledge for the damage and devastation that sexual assault brings. It is with deep regret that I say the church is one of the worst places to go for help. That's a hard thing to say, because I am a very conservative evangelical, but that is the truth. There are very, very few who have ever found true help in the church..."[18]

---

[18] http://www.christianitytoday.com/ct/2018/january-web-only/rachael-denhollander-larry-nassar-forgiveness-gospel.html?share

CHAPTER FOUR: BREAKING FREE

You can't hurt me now
I got away from you, I never thought I would.
—Madonna, "Oh Father"

By the power of the Spirit,[1] you come to know the love of the Father[2] and embrace the gospel—that good news that your sins are forgiven by the death, burial, and resurrection of the Son.[3] Further, your life grows to reflect a genuine heart for God—one that evidences your claim to be a follower of Jesus Christ.

That's what it means to become a Christian. And miraculously, despite the church, that's what I became.

My story of breaking free and getting away began in my fifteenth year and involved, among other things, chess with my grandfather, a movie adaptation of *David Copperfield*, and a girl named Maria.

As a teenager and into young adulthood, I struggled with my ability to discern, or understand the importance of even having, a specific point in time that I personally responded to or "accepted" the gospel. My difficulty came from trying to combine my normal, unexciting, and gradual growth in belief—in a seriously dysfunctional church environment—with the dramatic change reflected in many conversion stories. The mixture of bad theology, scare tactics, and manipulation in Berachah didn't help either.

---

[1] John 3:3.
[2] 2 Corinthians 5:18-19.
[3] 1 Corinthians 15:1-4.

Chess with My Grandfather

It was my grandfather, my father's father—an agnostic and someone who was very dear to me—who helped me learn to think. He told me that the only reason I was a Christian was because I was born in America. If I was born in the Middle East, I'd be a Muslim. In other words, one's religious belief is determined more by geography and cultural conditioning than by the merits of the belief itself.

We played chess during my summers and, when I was fifteen, he gave me Bertrand Russell's *Ninety Reasons Why I am Not a Christian*. I read the book with interest. This was still during the Berachah years and before the pedophilia and other hidden abuse hit the fan. Pastor Janson also gave me a book by the late Henry Morris called *Science Speaks* to counter some of my grandfather's and Russell's arguments.[4] I learned from both books but found the arguments for Christianity stronger. It was my grandfather, however—more than any other person—who helped me cultivate my mind and learn courage to ask honest questions, convictions that are vital parts of my ministry today.

From a theological perspective, I've come to see that saving faith is more than intellectual assent. Even "the demons believe and tremble."[5] Becoming a Christian involves change or transformation: "Therefore if any man is in Christ, he is a new creature; the old things passed away; behold, new things have come."[6] For this reason, I've found it important to view my conversion experience through the lens of, not just when did I learn to think but, when did a change take place in my heart and actions? When did I begin to "hunger and thirst after righteousness?"[7] These are difficult questions for many who come to Christ early in life. That's why, in addition to the "change in belief" experiences

---

[4] My journey toward evolutionary creationism came later. See https://www.carpentertheologian.com/how-i-changed-my-mind-about-genesis-1-and-science-part-1-of-5/
[5] James 2:19b.
[6] 2 Corinthians 5:17.
[7] Matthew 5:6.

associated with my grandfather, I place considerable weight on several events that happened during a three-month period of the same year. If God hadn't mercifully and supernaturally intervened, my life would certainly have taken a different path.

A Girl Named Maria

I was working in Berachah's bus ministry to underprivileged families. Through this venture, I became acquainted with a Puerto Rican girl who was twenty, a mother of a five-year old, and very attractive. (As I recall, she looked a lot like Paz Vega's character in the Adam Sandler's movie, *Spanglish*.) She could speak very little English and for that reason I thought I would befriend and try to help her. We began to write each other notes. I hid hers in my wallet and tried to use my Dad's Spanish dictionary to interpret them. (My dad was fluent in Spanish.)

What began as an innocent friendship soon grew into romantic and physical attraction. One day when I went to visit her and her extended family on my bike, she—the experienced one—arranged for her family to leave and began to kiss me, unbuttoning my shirt. Although I don't wish to pin all the harshness of the following "bad-news-woman" stereotype on her personally, it was the kind of scenario Proverbs warns young men about:

> For the lips of an immoral woman are as sweet as honey, and her mouth is smoother than oil. But in the end she is as bitter as poison, as dangerous as a double-edged sword. Her feet go down to death; her steps lead straight to the grave. For she cares nothing about the path to life. She staggers down a crooked trail and doesn't realize it.[8]

Remarkably, although I had lain awake many nights fantasizing about what might happen between us, when things got real, I was afraid and left before anything happened.

During the time all of this was playing out (a fifteen-year-old boy getting involved with a twenty-year-old girl) some "mysterious" things began to take place. One day on my way to her house, my

---
[8] Proverbs 5:3-6, NLT.

bike tire went flat. I fixed it and the next day it went flat again. In fact, this happened three times in a row. It seemed there was an unseen hand prohibiting me from making some very bad choices. Internally the warning light had begun to blink and I felt the pull of two different forces: my sinful desires and the goodness of God. This intense struggle began to surface in severe stomach cramps. One night my father picked me up from work (I had a job at Jamesway Department Stores building bikes) and confronted me about the notes she had sent. How did he know?

The night before, I had left my wallet in my pants pocket and my mom found the notes as she was doing the laundry. She showed them to my dad who quickly discerned that her intentions were far more serious than I understood. When I got home, with much apprehension, I unloaded the whole story on my parents. I felt embarrassed but relieved. Knowing what I know now, I give my parents an "A" for how they handled this situation. They showed great understanding, kindness to all involved, and took appropriate measures to end any contact between us.

That night, as I lay in bed, I poured my heart out to God in gratefulness. His grace had saved me from a very dangerous predicament that could have altered the course of my life. I recalled a verse I had memorized as a child in Christian school: "Or do you show contempt for the riches of his kindness, tolerance and patience, not realizing that God's kindness leads you toward repentance?"[9] God's kindness had saved me from a predatory situation and led me to repentance and I would not show contempt. I've thanked God many times since for what He kept me from doing during this very vulnerable time in my life.

Although the May 10, 1975 *Burning Hell* experience still stands out as significant in my spiritual journey, I've come to see it was religious abuse and manipulation inflicted on a child. It wasn't God. In my own healing and detox from shame-based concepts of God and religion, I no longer use this as the cherry to top off my Christian "coming to faith" story. I've learned to call a spade a

---

[9] Romans 2:4.

spade. Despite any good intentions, it was spiritual malpractice.

Lethal church experiences notwithstanding, God broke into my world during my fifteenth year. That's when my relationship with God became real and intimate. It's also when I began to desire to read the Bible frequently and to take my faith seriously.

As I continued to grow, I became known among adults and peers alike as one who was serious about God. By God's grace, although I had plenty of struggles with sin, my high school years were largely "a long obedience in the same direction."[10] This poem I wrote during this time gives evidence of my early and maturing faith:

> I pray, Oh God, today I'll be
> A chosen vessel fit for thee;
> That all I do will be thy will
> With love for souls my heart You'll fill
> Help me to fight sin day by day
> To make my goal to stay away
> From Satan and his pleasures strong
> And fight the things I know are wrong
> Please God, forgive me when I fall
> And though my sins be great or small
> I know you view them as the same
> With thanks I pray in Jesus name
> *Amen.*

Heroes, Victims, and a Gift from My Dad

One of the few perks about Berachah's school was that we could earn "privilege" by getting all our work done and this meant that on certain designated afternoons, classic films were shown. One of those was the 1970 film adaptation of the legendary novel *David Copperfield* by Charles Dickens, colorfully interpreted and directed by Delbert Mann.

In the final scene, David Copperfield, walking along the beach

---

[10] This phrase is by Eugene Peterson who wrote a book with the same title.

and grieving the death of his friend Steerforth, begins to process his life's journey out loud. Reflecting back, he says:

> Life asks more of us, demands it. It's not enough to be talented… or beautiful… or even simply loving… we must be strong or else the gifts God sends us into the world with will just fade and wither with the first wind that blows on us… the best steel must go through the fire.

And then he has an epiphany that takes him back to the sentence Dickens' classic begins with: "Whether I shall turn out to be the hero of my own life, or whether that station will be held by anybody else, these pages must show." In walking along the shore, then, David Copperfield essentially asks, will I be the hero of my own life or the victim of it? This question arrested my attention and began to haunt me. Many of the scenes of abuse in the movie triggered memories of my own abuse. Would I be the hero of my own life or the victim of it? Concomitant with this event, some kind of steel began to form inside me—a strength and resilience that mysteriously seemed to grow alongside my heart for God. I realized at 15 that much of what Mr. and Mrs. Janson were saying was not from God. I resented their control and strongly resonated with songs like Billy Joel's "My Life."

Although all the Jansons' perversion and abuse had not yet been revealed, I wondered what my dad thought about all of Berachah's rules and control. I'd begun to spend more time with him, working in his new business when I wasn't in school, but he was hard to read. He didn't always seem happy, but he did seem to enjoy my company. Furthermore, he did his best to make it to all of my high school basketball games. Although my dad wasn't a big sports guy, we had played catch and Frisbee in the backyard on many occasions. We also got seriously into ping-pong when I was eleven or twelve, sometimes playing daily whenever he got home from work. The closeness my father and I shared is one reason I later loved the 2013 film *About Time*. Several times throughout the movie, the father and son are seen talking together while playing ping-pong. This simple setting provides cohesiveness for one of the movie's central themes: delight in the father-son relationship, an experience I tasted in my relationship with my dad in my later teens and early twenties.

In my early teens, however, due to his busyness with church and a new business, although my dad was physically present, he was often emotionally absent. Again, something huge happened, however, in my fifteenth year. My father opened up to me in a way he never had before. We enjoyed a tradition every Sunday night when my mom was at choir practice. We would go to the local Mister Donuts, each get a coffee and pastry, and then come back to the church parking lot to talk.

At this time, the manipulation of the church culture was getting more and more evident. I wanted to go to a certain college in Springfield, Missouri, but the pastor and his wife had their own ideas about my future and wanted me to go to a school close to home. I felt that it was none of their business, only my parents' and mine. My dad, who was normally passive and preferred the role of the silent victim, finally said in the parking lot, "If I were you, when you turn eighteen, I'd get as far away from this place as possible."

I was stunned. I had no idea he felt this way. It was the first time he treated me as a peer or adult, and it began a trusted friendship that grew and grew. So much so, that five years later, in 1986, when I was preparing to marry, I had a hard time deciding who would be my best man, my dad or my best friend. I ended up choosing my best friend, but the difficulty I had deciding shows just how close we were. This heart-to-heart friendship really started with my dad's empathy and decision to trust me with how he really felt.

The Jonestown Massacre

Just three years before this crucial conversation with my dad in the car, on Nov. 18, 1978, something happened in a South American jungle that changed the way many in that era viewed religion—especially religion led by dictator-types like Berachah's leaders, the Jansons. "Of the nearly 1,000 church members who began the day in Jonestown, a cult commune, only 33 survived to see the next day."[11]

Although I was only twelve at the time, I've never forgotten the horror of that event. Images of more than 900 bodies in colorful clothes strewn across a landscape that looked otherwise like the setting of a benign Methodist camp-meeting. But what happened that day shouldn't be associated with church ladies and Sunday School picnics. It was the result of a deranged religious leader named Jim Jones who used his charisma and spiritual influence to destroy children, families, marriages, and adults that let other people think for them. They literally drank the Kool-Aid-like substance in such a tragic way it's hard to write about forty years later.

As I look back, I believe the Jonestown Massacre planted a seed of caution in my subconscious that grew into an alarm in my fifteenth year. This was related to a verse I had been forced to memorize as a child—one Pastor Janson repeated often to keep his congregation in line. Today, it still triggers discomfort and, for me, it's one of the scarier verses in the Bible:

> Obey them that have the rule over you, and submit yourselves: for they watch for your souls, as they that must give account, that they may do it with joy, and not with grief: for that is unprofitable for you.[12]

The verse frightens me because of words like "obey," "rule," and "submit" being attached to religious leaders, especially given realities like Jonestown or Berachah.

As I mentioned, following whatever God did in my heart after the Maria incident, I began to read the Bible voraciously. I started to notice that whenever God mentioned leaders or elders, it was almost always more than one. At fifteen, even before I knew what a "plurality of leadership" or a Presbyterian form of government was, I began to see that Berachah's one man and woman show did not fit what Scripture taught. As one who still believes that the Bible properly interpreted is a gift from God, I've thought deeply about

---

[11] For a thumbnail history of exactly what took place on Nov. 18, 1978, see this CNN fact
sheet: http://www.cnn.com/2008/US/11/12/jonestown.factsheet/index.html
[12] Hebrews 13:17, KJV.

Hebrews 13:17 for years. It is true that a church defined biblically is "a group of believers banded together for worship, edification, service, fellowship, and outreach; **accepting spiritual leadership**; willing to minister to all segments of society through the various gifts in the body;" and regularly receiving and administering the sacraments.[13] That's why any celebration of a "church-free" Christianity is problematic. I think there are some key insights in the verse itself, however, to show what "accepting spiritual leadership" is and isn't. These insights are essential in order to avoid the catastrophic harm that comes from blind obedience to church leaders.

- "They *watch* for your souls"—Watching implies action, attentiveness, vigilance, and a virtuous concern for your well-being. If these words don't describe your pastor, elders, or leaders, you're not in safe place.
- "They must give *account*—Accountability to God or wise people who care about you is a good thing in and of itself. Another way of saying this is: good and wise friends and leaders who watch your back or, in the context of the church, watch for your soul are a blessing. Think parents, guardians, and mentors. It's good to have people in our lives that help us choose the better angels of our nature. In fact, as this passage teaches, church leaders themselves are under authority and accountable to God. Thus, a willingness to be in accountable relationships including voluntary submission to the loving, reflective, biblical leadership in a local church can be a gift.[14]
- "**Do it with *joy*, not with *grief*.**"—This implies leaders who value emotions, are gentle, empathize, and show kindness, love, and support. It implies warmth, acceptance, grace, and sensitivity. Biblical leaders always put the well-being and needs of individuals and families over church

---

[13] I've adapted this definition from one David Dockery gave at a class I took at Southern Seminary.
[14] Proverbs 27:6, 17.

programs and pastoral ambitions. If the vibe or actions of a church's leadership on the whole are inaccessible, authoritarian, cold, rigid, or harsh, your church is not a place to thrive and grow. One friend who reviewed this project was concerned that some might be tempted to put up with a cold, overly strict church because "at least it's not abusive." Having learned the hard way in this area, here is his advice: "Do yourself a favor, give yourself permission to leave, and then leave. Find somewhere better. Save your low standards for the DMV, not the Church."

- "***Have* the rule over you**."—*Have* implies a state of being which, in the case of church authority, began with a voluntary association. Unless you're a child, your church membership is something you chose. Never give up *your* responsibility to think for yourself. If you believe the leadership of your local church is toxic, again, GET OUT. Go love God and join a life-giving expression of his church somewhere else.
- "**Obey *them*"**—Notice it doesn't say "obey the one man or woman." It says obey *them*.[15] Again, this reflects the safety of shared leadership through a plurality of elders, rather than one head, solo pastor who is over everyone else. Only Jesus Christ is the Head of the church. Moreover, he—the one whose yoke is easy and burden light—is the Good Shepherd who leads his churches through his Word and the reflective leadership of a plurality of godly men and women.[16]

God has entrusted pastors, elders, and deacons with *servant* leadership.[17] It should never be carried out in a heavy-handed manner. Acts 6:1–7 gives a wonderful picture of leadership working hand-in-hand together with a congregation. Elders should be free

---

[15] See also Eph. 1:22; 4:15; 5:23; Col. 1:18; 1 Cor. 11:3.
[16] Regarding women in church leadership, see what I have written here: https://www.carpentertheologian.com/women-in-church-leadership-part-1/
[17] Mark 10:45.

to set and guard the vision of the church (trusted and allowed to do what they were asked), leading gently but courageously. Wise leadership fosters congregants that are informed, thoughtful, and not afraid to share their true thoughts and feelings. In *The Leadership Challenge,* James Kouzes and Barry Posner write, "Leaders involve, in some way, all those who must live with the results."

I hope that telling my story of how I became a Christian despite the church might save many from an abusive, soul-killing ordeal like my family experienced at Berachah. I also pray that any places of worship that you join will be safe-guarded by intelligent and loving leadership teams that are part of a larger healthy, grace-based church family. (More on grace-based vs. shame-based church families in chapter seven.)

Finally, I pray that any hurts, tears, and pain associated with bad religion would give you greater discernment and judgment, yet not cause you to throw the baby out with the bath water. In the next three chapters, I'll share more stories and perspectives that have helped me heal, including those areas where I still walk with a limp, or that have caused me to stagger like Tolstoy, as well as the most important lesson I'm still learning.

CHAPTER FIVE: HEALING MOVES

They can change their minds but they can't change me...
—Jim Croce, "I Got a Name"

    Sheryl Crow says, "every day is a winding road" and that's definitely been my experience in trying to move ahead, pursue dreams, and distance myself from roots tied to South Jersey's pines and, unfortunately, many sad and bitter memories.

    In the summer of 1982, just three years before Pastor Janson was arrested for child molestation, my parents finally got up the courage to leave Berachah. It wasn't easy as their lives were intertwined in various ministries and leadership roles. Others who had left had been blacklisted and so they knew their departure would have to be secretive and severing. Making sure the church was empty, they dropped off a letter, giving no reason for our family's departure. Of course, any reason would be used against them; however, giving no reason caused folks to invent some. Many of the rumors of why we left were cruel and we were shunned by those I thought were my extended family and friends. At seventeen, this hurt a lot—especially the lie that I had gotten a girl pregnant and that *this* was the real reason my parents left. We traced this fiction to a conversation I had with the Jansons' daughter about Maria. In true whisper-down-the-lane fashion, it had morphed from a beautiful story of God's mercy and unseen hand to a convenient way to slander our family.

Unexpected Love

Another challenge in leaving Berachah was that, during my freshman and sophomore years, I had worked hard to graduate a year early and this would now be my senior year. In order to finish with continuity and graduate on time, my parents needed to find another school that used the same Accelerated Christian Education (A.C.E.) curriculum that Berachah had used. Thankfully, they found one nearby and enrolled me in Fairton Christian Center Academy (FCCA).

Again, amidst major relational transition, I was hurting. The lies that I had gotten a girl pregnant tore deeply into my soul and I shared this with my new school's headmaster, Pastor Moore. He listened intently and with empathy. Later that week, we went for a walk outside the school building. He opened the book of Psalms and showed me several passages about how, in the face of lies and enemies, God guards our name and reputation. I don't remember the specific verses, but the effect brought healing.

Coming from a shame-based, legalistic, Baptist setting, I learned a lot from the Pentecostals at this Assemblies of God school. They loved me. They respected me. I saw in many of their eyes the love of Christ. They helped me feel God's love and read the Bible through a more relational and less rule-based lens. Failure was viewed as something you could learn from. Although we didn't agree on all points of doctrine (no speaking in tongues for me, please), they respected the authentic work of the Holy Spirit in me. We found common ground in statements like this from the late Keith Green: "The only true marks of the Baptism of the Holy Spirit in a person's life are holiness and love."[1]

Interestingly, of the small class of six who graduated with me, the majority today no longer appreciate their Christian roots at FCCA or, at least, *that* brand of Christianity. Some view their

---

[1] This was from a doctrinal statement included in notes from the album *So You Wanna Go Back to Egypt*.

educational experience as "Mickey Mouse."[2] For all of us, the steps we take after graduation—including those ordered by the Lord[3]—give us unique perspectives. Of course, my distinct lens is more like a locket over my heart. I open it and see the love of my life, Pamela C. Austen. It was at FCCA where we first met and became high school sweethearts. She entered my life in 1982, and just four years later, took my hand in marriage to follow and at times lead me in healing and pursuing God.

Wolves in Sheep's Clothing Exposed

On July 3, 1985, Pastor Janson, then forty-seven, was arrested at a Virginia hospital, where he was recovering from a suicide attempt, after evading out-of-state felony charges.[4] This was the result of trying to flee a nine-count indictment against him for sexually assaulting three teenage boys who were under his care from 1975 to 1983.[5] Most of the charges were related to "engaging in intimate sexual contact," and one was for inflicting "unnecessarily severe corporal punishment."[6]

Mrs. Janson was also indicted in the abuse on February 25, 1986. Her allegations date from 1976 to 1982 and were for "severe corporal punishment inflicted" and "child neglect by failing to respond to the sexual abuse her husband committed on the children."[7] One friend recounted that in the later years, after our family had left Berachah, Mrs. Janson even walked around her home with a horsewhip and everyone was fair game.

Although this might seem like an anticlimactic end to the Jansons' physical crimes, it was only the beginning of the devastation that would play out for years in the lives of those they had spiritually raped. Besides the tsunami of pain unleashed in the

---

[2] I am using this here to mean too easy, ineffective, or unimportant to be taken seriously.
[3] Psa. 37:23.
[4] Philadelphia Inquirer 6 July 1985.
[5] The Daily Journal 9 July 1985.
[6] The Central New Jersey Home News 26 Dec 1985.
[7] The Daily Journal 26 Feb 1986.

lives of the fosters, the Jansons' "ministry" encouraged and was a haven for parental beatings and psychological abuse among all member families. Berachah was now in ruins and left with a culture and reputation it would never recover from. (This despite several salvage attempts on the part of subsequent pastors and former members. Inconceivably, as you'll see, just four years later, I too went back to be a part of these efforts.)

In the post Janson era, children—now adults—would have to try to do life as victims of undiagnosed and untreated trauma. A few fragile marriages would end in divorce. Many disillusioned followers would come to a place where they no longer looked to God or a church for answers. Most, including myself, would spend decades trying to understand, heal, and unlearn all the warped ideas from Berachah.

Just eight days after Pastor Janson's arrest, I sat home alone gazing at a front-page newspaper photo of him being led off to jail, handcuffed and with his head bowed down in shame. An amateur guitarist, I was so moved, I wrote my first song:

> I remember the days of my childhood
> and the things that we used to do.
> And I remember how you stood beside me
> as you spoke of things that were true.
> I remember how they would accuse you
> of things that brought shame to your name.
> And I remember how I would defend you
> for your grief it too brought me pain.
> What is this that I hear? Oh, it just can't be true,
> For what they have said is admitted by you.
> And though now proven, it still is so hard to believe
> For love always hopes that it wasn't deceived.
> Oh, it's a sad song that I must now sing of your shame
> For the life that you lived it was only a game.
> Oh, my friend, why is it still when the hurt should be mine
> That I only can cry for you must be so blind.

As my poem reveals, at nineteen, I was still in la-la land about the gravity of Rev. Janson's crimes. My primary childhood pastor had fallen from an undeserved pedestal and, in truth, I was still in shock and denial. Further, I had no idea of the devastation he and his wife had brought to vulnerable children; that is, of the long-term impact of abuse on victims and the scars they carry for life.

A couple of years later, working as an apprentice carpenter, I would ask my boss to give a summer job to one of the former foster children Mr. Janson had abused. During our three months working together, we became closer and one day I got up the nerve to ask him, "Joe, how did he get you to let him do the things he did to you, or the things you did to him?" I waited, not sure if I should have asked the question, or if he would respond. Joe looked away but then said softy, "He said it was OK because in the Bible it says that Jesus loved his disciples." I couldn't believe it—I was so disgusted, and this revelation woke me up out of an idealized world to see the atrociousness of Mr. Janson's crime.

Shame and Repressed Memories

Shortly after—and now looking through less child-like lenses—I remembered a time when I was twelve or thirteen, alone in the passenger seat next to Pastor Janson as he was driving. He had taken me with him soul-winning and, all of a sudden, he took his hand and rested it on my leg. He didn't do anything, but he kept it there long enough that I began to feel uncomfortable. Thinking it was weird, I then glanced over and saw that his eyes were wild and tormented, as if he were wrestling with something. He eventually removed his hand and we continued riding in silence. I now believe, given what he was involved in during that time and knowing something about addictions, that given the right circumstances, I too could have been one of his victims. And, although I don't want to minimize the severe abuse some have experienced, in truth I was a victim.

Dan Allender, in his classic *The Wounded Heart* explains:

It seems that many people operate on the principle that

whatever happened to them was not abuse... Because of this kind of confusion..., it is imperative to have a clear definition: Sexual abuse is any contact or interaction (visual, verbal, or psychological) between child/adolescent and an adult when the child/adolescent is being used for the sexual stimulation of the perpetrator or any other person.[8]

Allender continues that there are "two broad categories of abuse: sexual contact and sexual interactions. *Sexual contact* involves any type of physical touch that is designed to arouse sexual desire (physical or psychological) in the victim and/or the perpetrator."[9]

Writing about the creepy memory above even now makes me feel a little violated—like I want to take a shower to wash off the spot where he touched me. How much more those who have been seriously violated? How do you ever feel clean?

You see, we can repent of sin, but what do we do with shame?

This is such a difficult question and quest when it comes to healing. I don't know all the answers, but I've learned that shame is related to the authority we give to a certain standard; that is, shame is self-referenced and can be either illegitimate or legitimate, depending on the situation.

- Illegitimate: We may feel shame when we should not.
- Legitimate: We may not feel shame when we should.[10]

Again, Allender is helpful in distinguishing between the two:

Shame is not an easy topic. It involves a universal experience most people would like to ignore, but it is also a complex concept. Shame can be the result of the exposure to sin, therefore legitimate and desirable. However, even the exposure of sin may provoke an experience of shame that is too intense and self-absorbing to be from God. On the other hand, much of the shame we experience is not due to the exposure of our sin, but the revelation of some deficiency (or better said,

---

[8] Dan B. Allender, *The Wounded Heart: Hope for Adult Victims of Sexual Abuse* (Colorado Springs: Navpress, 1990), 30.
[9] Ibid., 31.
[10] See Jeremiah 8:9,12 as an example.

perceived deficiency) in our dignity. The difference between illegitimate and legitimate shame is found in the object of the exposure. Legitimate shame exposes *depravity*, and illegitimate shame shines a light on some element of *dignity*.[11]

Allender says that "shame has been called by Jean-Paul Sartre a hemorrhage of the soul. It is an awful experience to be aware that we are seen as deficient and undesirable by someone whom we hope will deeply enjoy us."[12] Illegitimate shame, especially, makes us forget our dignity. We fail to remember that the creator of the universe loves us and has freed us from our sins by the blood of Christ. Further, that he has made all those who receive him "a kingdom, priests to his God and Father…"[13] Healing and the way back always involve remembering that, as in Jim Croce's lyric, *we have a name*.

We see this process of realization occur in the story of Simba in Disney's *The Lion King*. Influenced by the lies of his Uncle Scar, Simba left the paradisal existence associated with Pride Rock to wander the jungle and wastelands. Later confronted by the wise, albeit eccentric, baboon witch doctor named Rafiki (meaning "friend"), Simba comes to a riverbank where he looks down and sees both his and his late father, Mufasa's, reflections in the water. He then looks up in the sky and sees a vision of his father. His father, who loved him dearly, says, "Remember, you are more than what you have become." At this place of repentance, Simba turns from his shadow self, rejects the lies of his Uncle Scar, and returns to Pride Rock to embrace his destiny as the Lion King.

We now return to our earlier question, asking it even more pointedly: **"You can repent of your own sin but what do you do with shame from sins inflicted on you by others?"** Although many require therapy in sorting this out, the answer still involves "remembering". Because of the cross, those in Christ have a name. Here is how one respected counselor put it:

---

[11] Op.Cit., 48.
[12] Ibid., 48.
[13] Revelation 1:5-6, ESV. See also, John 1:12.

The person who labors under a false sense of shame and guilt because of the sins of others against her needs more than affirmation and boosts to her self-esteem. She needs to see that the cross clarifies that she is responsible only for her own sins, not the sins of others that have so deeply wounded her. God's view of sin lifts her shame and self-loathing by giving her an identity that is rooted in Christ, not in the evil she has experienced.[14]

Forgiveness

A couple of years after Pam and I got married, I received an unexpected call from one of the Janson's biological sons asking me to be in his wedding. Although I had not seen him in over five years, I knew if I complied, I would have to face his mom, Mrs. Janson. Although it had been his dad, Mr. Janson who went to prison as the child molester, it was Mrs. Janson that was associated with my most serious wounds.

Her words had been so damaging. What's more, the schizophrenic way she could seem to hate you in one moment and then love you in the next had been torturously unsettling in my adolescence. The Kate Murphy incident was the worst. Again, although her husband was the child predator that went to prison, it was she who had been the master manipulator and primary purveyor of my shame. In fact, I knew one person from Berachah that hated her so much that he often visualized killing her.

What would I do when I saw her? I didn't know. But for her son—my friend's sake, I decided to move forward by being part of the wedding, asking God to help me respond appropriately if and when the time came. When I did meet her at the rehearsal, I learned she was also trying to heal and move on. She had divorced Mr. Janson and had changed her name back to her maiden name. Although she didn't ask for forgiveness, I felt compassion and decided to give her a hug. For some reason, I wanted to forgive her.

---

[14] Timothy Lane and Paul Tripp, *How People Change* (Greensboro: New Growth Press, 2006), 23.

What can I say? As the bumper sticker says, "Shit Happens," but so does Grace. I think I thought at the time, "It takes a bigger man to overlook the hurt of another. I can do it. I will be the hero of my own life, not the victim of it."

Looking back, there's no doubt God helped me in that moment. I also believe I had no idea how much shame I still carried at the core my being. I've since learned that childhood wounds go deep and are not easily brushed aside with a bumper-sticker-cliché with a little theology tacked on. Many of us, years later, still walk with a limp because of shame.

When you've lived through serious abuse, true forgiveness is extremely difficult and can seem almost impossible. According to Barna Group, approximately "a quarter of practicing Christians know someone they can't or won't forgive."[15] It's also confusing, especially in how forgiveness relates to reconciliation. (I didn't have to worry about this with Mrs. Janson because I never expected to see her again.)

Several years ago, I read through Ralph Keyes' collection of writings of *Sons on Fathers* where he reflects on the frustration many children feel over the distance in their relationship to their fathers. I found it interesting that the common thread running through the stories was the almost excruciating need to understand, forgive, and reconcile. Keyes' separation of these three concepts—understand, forgive, and reconcile—is very insightful:

- Understand—What we can do ourselves without the help of the offender or abuser.
- Forgive—What we, with God's help, can do without the help or participation of the offender or abuser.
- Reconcile—What we can't do ourselves. Unlike understanding and forgiveness, it requires cooperation and change on the part of the other person.

So how does Scripture delineate the differences between understanding, forgiving, and reconciling? In quoting Jesus, Dr.

---

[15] "Go Figure: June, 2019." Christianity Today, Volume 63, Number 5 (June 2019): 17.

Luke (the gospel writer most known for his nuance and "orderly accounts") writes: "Pay attention to yourselves! If your brother sins, rebuke him, and **if he repents, forgive him**…" (Luke 17:3, ESV)

Although this passage is talking about the basics of following Jesus in shared community, it's important to note the timing of offering forgiveness and reconciliation. Here Luke adds the phrase "if they repent" to the command to forgive frequently.[16] The late J.C. Ryle notes that:

> This expression is remarkable. It doubtless cannot mean, that we are not to forgive men unless they do repent. At this rate there would be much bitterness kept alive. But it does mean that when there is no repentance or regret for an injury done, there can be no renewal of cordial friendship, or complete reconciliation between man and man.[17]

At first glance, it might appear that Dr. Luke views forgiveness as almost synonymous with reconciliation or reunion. But the requirement "if they repent" creates an important distinction, and gives some biblical foundation for the wisdom offered by the late Lewis Smedes:

> When a person close to us wrongs us, he throws up two obstacles between us. One of the obstacles is our sense of having been violated, which produces our anger, our hostility, our resentment. This is the obstacle that our forgiving removes. But only the person who wronged us can remove the other obstacle. And he can remove it only by repentance and, if need be, restitution.[18]

The parable of the prodigal or two sons in Luke 15 illustrates the principles and process vividly. We see that the son would not have known the father's forgiveness unless he came to his senses and returned home. Further, if the father had not been eager to forgive, the son would never have been restored.

We also need to keep in mind that often, especially in the New

---

[16] See also, Luke 17:4.
[17] J.C. Ryle, *Expository Thoughts on the Gospels, Vol. 2* (Grand Rapids, MI: Baker, Reprinted 207), 225.
[18] Lewis Smedes, *The Art of Forgiveness* (New York: Moorings, 1996), 26.

Testament, forgiveness and reconciliation are combined. Again, this is part of what causes confusion. In other words, forgiveness is often the first step in the reconciliation process—not something separate from reconciliation. And, as Luke 17:3 teaches, if the person who sinned against us is repentant, we should be open to repair the relationship (unless it is unwise and unsafe to do so, as in the case of a child predator). Forgiveness means we are not going to look at a person solely from the perspective of his or her sin against us. Here is a helpful analogy:[19] Think of a particular relationship like a building. A wound or offense (or series of them over several years) destroys, damages, or blows up the building. Forgiveness, then, is like the bulldozer that clears away the rubble left by the previous sin. The old building had become structurally unsafe. A new building or relationship—if there is repentance and if it is safe—can now be constructed through reconciliation.

Here are a few questions that help me evaluate my heart and work toward forgiveness:

- Am I still bitter toward her/him?
- Do I want them to pay more than is appropriate or more than justice requires? Regarding retribution, we need to be careful as forgiveness is not incompatible with justice. For example, being brought to justice and paying for serious crimes against children, as in the case of the Jansons, *is* God-honoring.
- Am I trusting God to be the avenger and vindicator, or am I trying to steer the outcome toward the most punitive end possible?
- Do I wish them well and pray for them?
- Again, when I think of her/him, is it synonymous with how he/she sinned against me?

Remember Keyes' three categories: Understanding is always possible. It does not require the other person(s). Forgiveness is also always possible, with God's help, and does not require relationship

---

[19] I first heard this analogy from Dr. Jeff Forrey in a doctoral class at Westminster Seminary.

with or cooperation from the other person(s) who wronged us. Reconciliation, however, requires repentance and change from all parties. Moreover, there are some situations where, even if this occurs, it is still not wise, safe, desirable, or possible to restore relationship. For the Christian, though, forgiveness is not an option.[20] We forgive out of obedience to Christ and for the sake of our own healing. As Anne Lamott well said, "Not forgiving is like drinking rat poison and then waiting for the rat to die."[21]

Therapy

It wasn't until 2003, as a thirty-seven-year-old pastor, that my healing progressed again in a major way—strangely through the catalyst of suffering and more emotional pain. I was serving a dear congregation in Willow Grove, Pennsylvania. I had been there since 1998 and the church had grown a lot until we hit some challenges. Finances, factions, false teaching, aging and weary leaders, good folks moving away, and my own inexperience and impatience all seemed to come together in a perfect storm. I began to feel like the little Dutch boy who did not have enough fingers for all the holes in the dike.

It was also an independent church, and so I had little outside support for help. Weekly preaching became almost unbearable, as I was having trouble pulling my soul up by the bootstraps to a place I just wasn't living. Emotionally, I was exhausted and I knew that, given my public role, I could no longer hide. I also began to experience more and more conflict in my relationship with Pam, and I didn't know where to turn. Thankfully, I learned about an excellent counseling agency nearby that gave a discount to clergy. Someone also gave a gift, and Pam and I began therapy with a wonderful, seasoned, theologically reformed Christian psychologist named Dr. Barbara Shaffer. We did some couples therapy, but it was the one-on-one counseling that had the biggest impact on my growth.

---

[20] Matthew 6:12-14.
[21] Anne Lamott, *Traveling Mercies: Some Thoughts on Faith* (1999).

After listening to me a ton and skillfully probing with questions to get at the heart of my issues, Dr. Shaffer gently confronted me about "despising my South Jersey roots." Up to this point, I lived with a lot of anger, bitterness, and resignation related to my small-town beginnings, parents' later divorce, and especially my early shame-based church formation. I remember what she said as if it were yesterday: "I don't know all the answers, Greg, but I do know that it's not right to despise your roots. If you believe in the sovereignty of God, you were born and raised in south Jersey for a reason." She was referring to something the Apostle Paul said in Acts 17:26:

> And he made from one man every nation of mankind to live on all the face of the earth, having determined allotted periods and the boundaries of their dwelling place....[22]

It's also a major theme in Joseph's story from the Bible. After his brothers' terrible abuse and lies that forced him into slavery and decades of suffering, and after God then raised Joseph up to become second in command in Egypt where he could have chosen to annihilate his brothers, he forgave them instead, saying, "You meant it unto me for evil but God for good."[23] That day, Dr. Shaffer introduced me to the ministry of Tim Keller via a four-part series on the life of Joseph. Keller's messages were extremely healing and this series is still my favorite today.

Singer-songwriter, Wes King's song "Joseph's Trouble" captures emotions and wisdom from the Joseph story well, offering hope and the possibility of meaning, even in our pain:

> They say time can heal the wounds we bare
> But time don't change what put them there
> When the memories stir it all up again
> It's hard to understand
> Joseph's trouble is trouble indeed
> So hard to let go what hurts so deep

---

[22] ESV. Words in bold, mine.
[23] Genesis 50:20.

How quickly we forget
God sees things we can't see yet
…there just might be some purpose in our pain.

CHAPTER SIX: SEXUAL STAGGERS

We are all in the gutter, but some of us are looking at the stars.
—Oscar Wilde

Finding purpose and a cure for pain are certainly gifts we can be grateful for, and even point others to along the road, but what about those stubborn sins, especially those related to our sexuality—that which is inextricably bound to who we are? Many of us can identify with Tolstoy's words from chapter four:

> Attack me, I do this myself, but attack me rather than the path I follow… If I know the way home and am walking along it drunkenly, is it any less the right way because I am staggering from side to side?[1]

Staggering is a good image as, for me, there's been no struggle that's tormented me more than trying to come to peace with my sexuality. Sorting out beliefs, emotions, desires, and actions related to illegitimate vs. legitimate shame, and sexual dignity vs. depravity have been my biggest challenges in being a Christian.

Christians don't like to talk about sex. In the church, even if sexual desire isn't seen as something dirty as it was at Berachah, it remains private and hidden. Although part of this is proper—talking about it too much can seem like TMI, not talking about it at all makes it difficult to deal with distortions and heal. More fundamentally, a church that doesn't talk enough (and appropriately) about sexuality is a root cause of the distortions in the first place. Since the church is the preeminent supporter of

---

[1] Phillip Yancey, *Soul Survivor* (New York: Doubleday, 2001), 130.

"every good and perfect gift" from God,[2] if it were to talk openly—getting this topic right from the beginning, maybe we wouldn't have so many adults in the church needing to sort through distortions later in life.

It is also certain that covering up problems only increases the amount of abuse. Millennials get this more than older generations: "According to a new study sponsored by LifeWay Christian Resources, 10 percent of Protestant churchgoers under 35 have previously left a church because they felt sexual misconduct was not taken seriously. That's twice as many as the 5 percent of all churchgoers who have done the same."[3] Revelations of sexual abuse have been coming to light for decades in the Catholic church and recently we learned about 700 victims in the Southern Baptist Convention (SBC), the largest Protestant denomination.[4] Clearly a less private, and more candid conversation is needed. And instead of avoiding that conversation, it's time to reclaim it.

The heinousness of child sexual abuse along with widespread cover-ups aside, when something so transcendent, powerful, and integral to our humanity remains misunderstood, many suffer in silence. Some might understandably be wondering, "Greg, what does all this have to do with your story of how you became a Christian despite the church?" The answer is that part of becoming a Christian means honoring God with our body.[5] Indeed, following Christ compels us to look at questions of purity and sexuality under His Lordship.[6] And *that's* why I've chosen to be brutally honest, transparent, and go more in depth in this chapter.

---

[2] James 1:17.
[3] https://lifewayresearch.com/2019/05/21/churchgoers-split-on-existence-of-more-sexual-abuse-by-pastors/
[4] https://www.houstonchronicle.com/news/investigations/article/Southern-Baptist-sexual-abuse-spreads-as-leaders-13588038.php
[5] 2 Corinthians 12:21; Galatians 5:16-24.
[6] Although answering this and other related questions is beyond the capacity of this book, see this excellent statement on human sexuality from the Evangelical Presbyterian Church: http://epcoga.wpengine.com/wp-content/uploads/Files/1-Who-We-Are/B-About-The-EPC/Position-Papers/PositionPaper-HumanSexuality.pdf

Living in a sexually saturated culture, I want Christian discipleship to address the reality of where we live and some of our toughest questions. Like, what is part of legitimate freedom God gives and what is not? What is a biblical sin and what is a cultural sin? What is a perversion of holy desire and what is just religious baggage? Are my desires for pleasure from God, or do they separate me from God?[7] What is normal and beautiful, and what is disordered and harmful? What is pornography and what is art? And even if we identify clear answers to these questions, what do we do with our desires that often seem at odds with God's intent? If becoming a Christian is not about God fulfilling our every desire but giving us better ones, how do we change? Or, to ask this later question a different way that reflects the pain of many…

Why Can't I Change?

As a carpenter, it's no secret I've installed a lot of windows. The time I jumped out of one, however, is something I've rarely shared.

The Christian faith teaches that the ground is level at the foot of the cross and evangelism—at its best—is just one beggar showing another beggar where the bread is. We all have our sins and, like most labradors I've owned, have a strange love for trash. Sometimes we know we need to get our shit together and sometimes a close friend is kind enough to highlight this fact. Though none of us likes to see our true selves in the mirror, confrontation with the reality of our mess can be a gift if it brings greater self-awareness, repentance, and change. But how? Where is the locus for change?

At 17, as a disciple of Keith Green, a passionate Christ-follower and singer-songwriter who I discovered through my high school friends, I resolved to just try harder, as I resonated with Keith's lyrics: "My flesh is tired of seeking God, but on my knees I'll stay. I want to be a pleasing child until that final day."[8] Despite

---

[7] See Hebrew 11:25.
[8] Keith Green, *Songs for the Shepherd*, 1982.

all my effort, though, I could not pray hard enough, or make vows strong enough to extricate myself from my impurity. Added to this, I had not yet had time to detox from Berachah's warped ideas about God, and all their attempts to motivate with guilt, fear, and shame. I had so much angst and psychological turmoil.

For example, I remember, back in the early eighties, watching *Raiders of the Lost Ark* at home with my family. I had been wrestling with my sexuality and trying intensely to please God. There was a scene toward the end of the movie where Indy grabs the female lead's hand and—in the nick of time—saves her from falling into a pit. There, suspended in mid-air, legs dangling and—with the camera focused below—you could see her underwear. Honestly, it was an innocuous scene by today's standards, but it triggered my inner "demons." Caring deeply about God, I wanted desperately to be holy and pure. It's as if I wanted to eradicate sexual desire from my being. After the movie, I went in my room, opened the second story window of our bi-level, and jumped. I hit the ground and then went running as fast as I could into the woods. Tormented, with my arms up shielding my face from the branches, I ran until I could run no more.

As you can probably guess, I returned home the same man: whole and broken, intact and fragmented, and still the same mix of vices and virtues.

Thankfully, after years of severe mental distress and self-loathing, I no longer believe God is obsessed with our genitals. That is, I no longer believe he's like Sauron—the all-seeing eye in *The Lord of the Rings*—or *1984*'s "Big Brother" constantly watching our sexual urges with hyper-vigilance, becoming angry and disgusted whenever we masturbate. Yes, God cares about our thought life, but I'm with those who believe that occasional masturbation that focuses on the pleasure of the body and not lustful relationships or images can be preventative and even beneficial.[9]

---

[9] For seven varied but helpful perspectives on this controversial and much-avoided topic, see https://rachelheldevans.com/blog/christians-masturbation

The Christian Foundation for Sexual Healing

More importantly, I've learned that—even in our sin and addictions, gutters can help us find God. The flesh consistently fails, the God who created the stars…saves. Jesus died to justify the ungodly; therefore, we have hope![10] I now understand that the Holy Spirit is working in me "both to will and to do of his good pleasure."[11] In fact, often he must work in me "to will" before he works in me "to do:" That is not a cop-out but a huge comfort. What's more, the Spirit transforms our heart and desires so that we do change over time, from the inside-out. And so, friend, as St. Benedict of Nursia said, "Never despair of God's mercy." Our failures are meant to point us to our continuing need to cast ourselves on God's mercy.

The "fear of the LORD may be the beginning of wisdom,[12] but God's normal MO is to overwhelm us with his goodness and kindness:

> Do you despise the riches of his kindness and forbearance and patience? Do you not realize that God's kindness is meant to lead you to repentance? But by your hard and impenitent heart you are storing up wrath for yourself on the day of wrath, when God's righteous judgement will be revealed. For he will repay according to each one's deeds: to those who by patiently doing good seek for glory and honor and immortality, he will give eternal life.[13]

Again, it is his goodness that leads to repentance. This is the same passage I had memorized as a child—the one God used to arrest my attention when my bike tire kept going flat while I was trying to see Maria. In the verses above, we learn it is the loving Father God with outstretched arms, not the policeman God with billy club, that melts our icy hearts. We are faithless, yet he remains faithful.

---

[10] Romans 4:5.
[11] Philippians 2:13, KJV.
[12] Proverbs 1:7.
[13] Rom. 2:4-7, ESV.

But someone will ask, what about the rest of this passage? Don't the verses that follow Romans 2:4 say it is "our deeds" and "doing good" that are the basis of God's payment or the condition of the gift of eternal life? That's a great question and here is the nuance needed to cut through the fog of the works/grace debate: The Scripture teaches that all of our works are *by* the enlivening Spirit[14] and are themselves gifts of grace.[15] The work is begun and fueled by God, but is carried out through works we ourselves do.[16] It's synergistic cooperation.

But here's the critical point: Yes, there's synergy, but God alone possesses the power to change us. We must rely fully on Him.

In order to grow in Christ, it's imperative that we avoid the error in the Galatian church:

> Oh, foolish Galatians! Who has cast an evil spell on you? For the meaning of Jesus Christ's death was made as clear to you as if you had seen a picture of his death on the cross. Let me ask you this one question: Did you receive the Holy Spirit by obeying the law of Moses? Of course not! **You received the Spirit because you believed the message you heard about Christ.** How foolish can you be? After starting your Christian lives in the Spirit, why are you now trying to become perfect by your own human effort?[17]

After we left Berachah, a critical moment in my spiritual growth occurred when I first heard a sermon on this passage in my late teens. The struggle with masturbation and pornography had been unbearable. The bolded section of the Galatians passage above taught me and still reminds me that *the power* for sanctification, what some call "perfecting," comes in believing the gospel message more deeply, not in human effort. Yes, sexual purity requires intentionality, but it's a grace-fueled pursuit; it's not about perfection.

Berachah taught that if I employed enough strategies, rules, or

---

[14] Ephesians 2:1.
[15] Ephesians 2:8-9.
[16] Philippians 2:12b-13.
[17] Galatians 3:1-3, NLT.

"eight musts," I would impress or please God. It was *self*-reliance and *self*-righteousness—things that God calls "filthy rags" no matter how pure the behavior looks externally.[18] On the other side of Berachah, I've had to continually learn to repent of seeing *my* effort, *my* flesh, as the primary catalysts for change. Isaiah 30:15 says it well:

> This is what the Sovereign LORD, the Holy One of Israel, says: "In repentance and rest is your salvation, in quietness and trust is your strength…"

Instead of striving to please God, becoming a Christian means learning *first*—every day and always—to trust and rest in the power of God to change us from the inside out. *His* righteousness, mercy, and power are our only Hope. That nuance makes all the difference in the motivation behind our efforts.

Five Strategies for Fighting Lust

Having laid the essential Christian foundation for a pursuit of sexual healing, I now want to share five practical strategies that have helped me the most in fighting lust:

- **Foresight:** Make choices in moments of strength to prepare for moments of weakness. For example, if you are tempted to look at porn at a certain time of day on your iPhone, consider giving it to a trusted friend to hold ahead of time. That way, you won't have access to it when you're tempted. You can also have someone set restrictions on your phone via your provider to turn off cellular and web capabilities at certain times of the day.[19] If certain cable channels are an issue, try to get a package that doesn't include them. The idea here is to creatively and proactively prepare at times when you aren't tempted for times when you will or may be.
- **Replacement and distraction:** Sexual temptation doesn't decrease by focusing on the struggle. Instead, it decreases in intensity by finding another hobby or passion to give

---

[18] Isaiah 64:6.
[19] Some parents do this with their kids' phones.

yourself to. This strategy is similar to the question "how do you *not* think about the color green?" The answer? By thinking about red or another color instead. Ephesians 4:28 hints at this strategy in its promotion of work and sharing as an antidote to stealing: "Anyone who has been stealing must steal no longer, but must work, doing something useful with their own hands, that they may have something to share with those in need." (NIV)

- **Confession to safe people:** Catholics stress the importance of regular confession of sin to human beings (in their case, a priest), not just God. Protestants love to quote 1 Timothy 2:5 to say that we don't need to confess our sins to a priest because we can go to directly to God. They are often content to ignore, however, James 5:16, which says, "Therefore, confess your sins to one another and pray for one another, that you may be healed." Catholics, even if one doesn't agree with their confessional system, at least provide a safe place for the confession of sin to other caring human beings. In contrast, my experience at Berachah taught me to hide my faults, act as spiritual as possible, and judge others with problems. There was no safe place or encouragement to be real with people. I now prioritize honest, safe one-on-one relationships, and in small groups (more on these in the next chapter). Yes, thank God, we can go directly to the Father through Jesus,[20] but we still need to be real about our faults and struggles with appropriate, safe brothers or sisters—faithful friends—who serve us in a priestly role. This is especially important with sexual addictions, as their strength is in secrecy.
- **The H.A.L.T. acronym from Alcoholic Anonymous (AA):** I learned this powerful strategy from a former morphine addict who, when I first met him, had been clean seven years thanks to AA. The strategy here is to identify your trigger; that is, one of the four main times you are more

---

[20] Again, 1 Timothy 2:5; see also Hebrews 4:16.

likely to cave to a given temptation: **H**ungry, **A**ngry, **L**onely, and **T**ired. You then use this learning and awareness to "halt" and be more vigilant in standing strong in times you are most vulnerable.[21]

- **Regular church attendance and the Lord's Supper:** Although I flex with the custom of a particular church, I prefer weekly communion as it's one of the easiest ways to make a service more Christ-centered. Further, it promotes regular examination and repentance. On the practical need for regular church attendance and related disciplines, I've also benefited from this great quote by the late Bishop J.C. Ryle:

    Sanctification, again, is a thing which depends greatly on a diligent use of Scriptural means. When I speak of 'means,' I have in view Bible-reading, private prayer, regular attendance on public worship, regular hearing of God's Word, and regular reception of the Lord's Supper. I lay it down as a simple matter of fact that no one who is careless about such things must ever expect to make much progress in sanctification. I can find no record of an eminent saint who ever neglected them. They are appointed channels through which the Holy Spirit conveys fresh supplies of grace to the soul, and strengthens the work which He has begun in the inward man. Let some call this… [legalistic] if they please, but I will never shrink from saying there are no 'spiritual gains without pains.' I should as soon expect a farmer to prosper in business who contented himself with sowing his fields and never looking at them till harvest, as expect a believer to attain much holiness who was not diligent about his Bible-reading, his prayers, and the use of his Sundays. Our God is a God who works by means, and He will never bless the soul of that man who pretends to be

---

[21] 1 Peter 5:7.

so high and spiritual that he can get on without them.[22]

Navigating Mid-life and the Empty Nest

As we get older, God continues to work in us "to will and to do of his good pleasure." He takes us further, higher, and deeper and often we find that, as singer-songwriter Jon Foreman says, "the wound is where the light shines through."[23]

In wrestling through my issues and preparing to write this book, I found that, although I was now over fifty and believed the gospel to my core, I still couldn't relax. Many of the questions we began this chapter with related to shame, repression, and desire were still confusing, and I wasn't comfortable in my own skin. Enjoyment, getting lost in a moment—these were very difficult for me. I felt secure in the love of Christ. I wasn't trying to earn salvation or obtain merit. I believed in the free grace of a Sovereign God and the finished work of Christ. And, I knew I couldn't add anything to divine gifts of salvation from hell, sonship, and friendship with God. I got all that.

What I continued to struggle with was how my sex-drive was connected to whatever remained of my overall fire, motivation, and uniqueness. Desire—not just for sex but to do anything—tells us we're not dead. We're still alive and we've got something to give. How was I to consistently channel my passions in positive, productive, and God-honoring directions?

Entering the empty-nest season only exacerbated the struggle as, with no kids around, I either had to grow with Pam, or go underground. Of course, it's human nature to hide and blame, and although my modus operandi isn't often to blame, it is to hide. Hiding means you communicate less, not more, making an already uncomfortable relational dynamic unbearable. Kids provide a buffer, a distraction from marital issues either known or unknown.

---

[22] J. C. Ryle, *Holiness* (Cambridge & London: James Clarke & Co., Reprinted 1956), 20-21.
[23] This is the name of the title track off Switchfoot's album, *Where the Light Shines Through*, 2016.

When they're gone, it's just the two of you night after night. In the silence, the space between you and any walls in your relationship become painfully obvious.

That's why some couples get divorced or pursue separate worlds. Regarding the latter option, loneliness becomes the tradeoff for stress and tension. And, if both partners love God, it's a way to technically guard the sanctity of marriage, a picture of God's covenant love, and avoid divorce—something that more often than not, hurts children, and takes an axe to legacy.[24]

In marriage and family ministry over the years, this is where I've seen addictions and justifications related to pornography resurface; that is, as a way to check out of emotional pain, difficulty, or uncomfortableness.

Or, I've seen it play out in the opposite direction: Sometimes it's easier to take something we feel is dangerous or can't handle—like our sexuality—and shove it in a box, lock it, and bury it deep in the ground. The problem is these word pictures—shove, lock, bury—are fantasies because the desire and any impurity mixed with it is inside us. It's not external. It's part of the core of who we are—our heart and soul, our DNA. It's in our very blood. That's why repression is not the answer.

So what *is* the answer and how can we navigate mid-life and the empty nest years in such a way that we end up with greater intimacy and enjoyment with our spouses rather than drifting apart?

---

[24] See especially Judith S. Wallerstein and Julia M. Lewis, "The Unexpected Legacy of Divorce: Report of a 25-Year Study," *Psychoanalytic Psychology* 21, no. 3 (2004): 353–370, accessed November 14, 2016, http://www.fellowshipoftheparks.com/Documents%5CUnexpected_Legacy_of_Divorce.pdf. This follow-up study of 131 children, who were 3–18 years old when their parents divorced in the early 1970s, marks the culmination of 25 years of research. The use of extensive clinical interviews allowed for exploration in great depth of their thoughts, feelings, and behaviors as they negotiated childhood, adolescence, young adulthood, and adulthood. At the 25-year follow-up, a comparison group of their peers from the same community was added. Described in rich clinical detail, the findings highlight the unexpected gulf between growing up within an intact versus divorced family, and the difficulties children of divorce encounter in achieving love, sexual intimacy, and commitment to marriage and parenthood.

Here are nine things that have helped me the most to date:
- Stop being passive and come out of your cave. Proverbs 18: 1 says, "Whoever isolates himself seeks his own desire; he breaks out against all sound judgment." (ESV)
- Lean into God; seek his power to repent, listen, and forgive, as well as to be kind, vulnerable, and honest. Thank him for his steadfast love in your trouble.[25]
- Channel the fire that is you (your sexuality, motivations, passions—all of it) into the good works God has created you for. Get a handle on your gifts and make the most your "talents" to His glory. Don't bury your specialness; rather, believe he is good and worthy of your investment.[26]
- View each other as good-hearted people. Extend grace to your spouse and yourself.
- Stay steady and try not to take everything personally.
- Be realistic: healing doesn't happen without lots of talking, tears, and time. Many have found that it takes weeks, months, even years to become fully aware of a hurt or the root of a particular wound. Be patient with each other; you're in it for the long haul.
- If you're stuck, get help.[27]
- Love your kids and grandkids well, determine to have their backs, but don't center your lives around them. Put your marriage and relationship first. Spend time together. Rediscover whimsy. Explore, take walks, exercise. Take on a shared mission or project. Identify ways to love, give, and sacrifice together.
- Encourage one another. Play to each other's strengths and remember as C.S. Lewis said, "you're never too old to set a new goal or dream a new dream." Find ways to follow

---

[25] James 4:6-10, Psalm 107, Rom. 8:39.
[26] Ephesians 2:10; Matthew 25:14-30.
[27] You can find a counselor near you that is connected with the American Association of Christian Counselors here:
https://connect.aacc.net/?search_type=distance

this advice both separately and together.

In embracing all that's been said above, especially as is relates to personal and marital purity, we also need to add nuance to our apologetic against pornography.

Getting Our Apologetic Against Pornography Right

For twenty-five years, many of us have laughed through or in spite of Joey and Chandler's regular consumption of porn on *Friends*. And today, former *Baywatch* babe and Playmate, Pamela Anderson, is a "strange" outlier because, now that she's gotten rich and famous off of being objectified—yet, seeming to have learned the hard way, she speaks out about pornography as "corrosive" and "a public hazard."[28] Meanwhile, America's darling couple and famed celebrities of *The Voice*, Gwen Stefani and Blake Shelton, celebrate the fact that they "watch porn, cookin' shows, and Instagram" after they put the kids to bed.[29]

Despite this "boys will be boys," no-shame-no-stigma, it's-perfectly-fine-in-an-exclusive-relationship sea change, pornography is still the crack-cocaine of the soul—a real drug-of-choice that has the power to kill and destroy individuals and relationships. In living in a culture that increasingly seeks to normalize porn, it's important to make sure we know *why* it's wrong and base our biblical case against it on the right passages. That's why using the text below as our primary apologetic is problematic:

> "But I say unto you that everyone who looks at a woman with lust has already committed adultery with her in his heart."[30]

Despite writing before the internet and iPhones, the late John White gave some thoughtful and valuable guidance on the proper

---

[28] https://www.telegraph.co.uk/news/2016/09/01/pamela-anderson-urges-men-to-give-up-pornography-describing-it-a/ See also https://www.foxnews.com/entertainment/pamela-anderson-claims-weve-lost-many-good-men-to-porn-and-playstation-in-odd-twitter-thread

[29] https://www.usmagazine.com/celebrity-news/news/blake-shelton-jokes-about-watching-porn-with-gwen-stefani/

[30] Matthew 5:28, NRSV.

application of this passage and its relation to porn:

> I would like to make a distinction here… It seems to me that it is one thing to allow my fantasies to be stirred by the cover of a pornographic magazine [or internet site] and something altogether different to allow myself to play lustfully with the idea of having a relationship with a flesh and blood man or woman that I know personally. Both activities are fantasy activities. Yet it seems to me that in Matthew 5 it is the second issue that Jesus is talking about.
>
> I must be careful to not make too much of this distinction for in real life it is less clear-cut…. Half-way between the nude in Penthouse or Playgirl [or internet site] and the person I know in real life comes the girl in the bikini on the beach. The girl in the magazine is not (to me) a person. But then neither, for that matter is the bikinied body on the beach.
>
> Yet the distinction remains an important one. Sexual fantasy stimulated by pornography are purely erotic fantasies. They have to do with physical, animal arousal only. The masturbating adolescent, obsessed with the breasts of a pinup and torn with an urge in his groin is thinking primarily of his own physical feelings and his desire to relieve them. But the sexually experienced man or woman (whether young or old), those who know what is involved with a sexual relationship and especially those who may be involved in an unsatisfactory marriage relationship, are in a different position. Their prime preoccupation is with the grass in another meadow which seems greener than the grass in their own. Or else it may be the man or woman who has no pasture but covets what belongs to another. John speaks of "the lust of the eyes," the desire to possess beautiful things. Lust exists where our desires are our masters rather than our servants. So that to lust after a woman has a broader meaning than merely to experience erotic arousal or fantasies.
>
> I am not seeking to justify playing around with sexually stimulating fantasies. To play around with sexual fantasies is a miserable, guilt-evoking, lonely travesty of sex. I do not

believe, however, that sexual fantasies in general are what Jesus is talking about… He is talking rather about coveting another person's spouse, or else someone known to me whom I may not possess.[31]

Again, White's nuance is valuable. Yet given our tendency to justify ourselves and rationalize away our sin, we must adopt a better, more intellectually and emotionally formidable case against pornography.

I propose this. In entering the virtual world of pornography, one decides to join with and give a piece of his or her heart to a gigantic industry of distorted desire, exploitation, abuse, and voyeuristic using.[32] Pornography is a willing or forced defacing of the image of God, a disfiguring of the transcendent beauty and pleasure of the sexual experience. It dissipates and derails human potential; it distracts from and deadens holy desire.[33]

In pursuing purity, loving God with our minds, and better using Scripture to help stand against, flee from, and eradicate porn and any other sexual sin from our lives, here are several passages I have found exceptionally meaningful:

- A great verse from Job: "I made a covenant with my eyes not to look lustfully at a young woman." (31:1, NIV)
- Some excellent prayers from the Psalms:
    - "I will walk with integrity of heart within my house; I will not set before my eyes anything that is base." (101:2b-3a, NRSV)
    - "Turn my eyes from looking at vanities; give me life in your ways." (119:37, NRSV)
    - "Let your steadfast love become my comfort…" (119:76a, NRSV)
    - "Don't let me drift toward evil or take part in acts

---

[31] John White, *Eros Defiled* (Downers Grove, IL: IVP, 1977) 94-95.
[32] I am thinking here of "heart" as it is used in Proverbs 4:23: "Above all else, guard your heart…" The heart in scripture is the center of our passion—the seat of our mind, will, and emotions.
[33] For research on the negative affects of pornography, see http://truthaboutporn.org/study/ .

of wickedness. Don't let me share in the delicacies of those who do wrong… I look to you for help, O Sovereign LORD. You are my refuge; don't let them kill me. Keep me from the traps they have set for me, from the snares of those who do wrong. Let the wicked fall into their own nets, but let me escape. (141:4, 8-10, NLT)

- My favorite from the Apostle Paul: "Now in a great house there are not only vessels of gold and silver but also of wood and clay, some for honorable use, some for dishonorable. Therefore, if anyone cleanses himself from what is dishonorable, he will be a vessel for honorable use, set apart as holy, useful to the master of the house, ready for every good work. So flee youthful passions and pursue…love…. (2 Timothy 2:20-22, ESV)

CHAPTER SEVEN: LEARNING TO LOVE

There are wounds time will not wash clean if we stood here forever in the rain. I believe when we turn around and learn to love, finally we find ourselves again.[1]
—Randy Stonehill

When it comes to becoming a Christian, the apostle Paul says that love is the crème de la crème of virtues: "If I could speak all the languages of earth and of angels, but didn't love others, I would only be a noisy gong or a clanging cymbal."[2] Knowing this and given my "deformative" church experience, I've thought deeply on the beautiful lyric above for thirty years. Because it captures so many of our stories and provides great wisdom, I'll use it to help structure the content of this chapter. Before we explore its' main phrase "learn to love," I'd like to comment on the prior phrase "turn around."

Managing Our Own Store

I once heard Dr. Laura Schlessinger say, "You can't drive through life looking through your rearview mirror." Yes, there is a place for looking back at the past and seeking understanding. This can lead to self-awareness and certainly our biological and spiritual families have great influence on us. In other words, the effects of good and bad parenting matter. There comes a point, however,

---

[1] "The History in Your Eyes" from the album *Until We Have Wings*, 1990.
[2] 1 Corinthians 13:1, NLT.

where we need to make a choice to turn around, move on, and learn to love. Learning to love starts with a decision to take personal responsibility for our life. It's a choice to embrace both courage and dignity. We ask, as in *David Copperfield*, "Will I be the hero of my life or the victim of it?" Again, it's good that you can now connect the dots between something you feel or do and something that happened to you. Identifying and naming these kinds of things *is* an important step related to self-awareness and healing. But the time comes when you have to think about *your* name, and *your* responsibility to sit in the control booth of your own life and move on. No more excuses. Someone has said that excuses are the crutches of the uncommitted.

Think of it this way: Imagine you inherited a store that had been mismanaged for years and thus had a bad reputation in the community. For the first year or so, as you worked to restore its reputation and give it a new name, you might legitimately blame any lack of progress on the previous owners. Customers would likely understand and give grace. There comes a point, however, when this approach is not going to work anymore. It's now *your* store connected to *your* name. What goes on in it on a daily basis is connected to you and you alone. In other words, no more excuses. The time has come and it's now your responsibility to manage your own store.

This is a difficult step in the healing process and requires therapy for many to get there. Additionally, it's not always a once and done step. You may take it initially and then find yourself entering a new place of growth where you need to take it again.

A book I once read demonstrated this clearly. It was a disturbing work of autobiographical fiction called *The Last Year of War* by Shirley Nelson. It's a psychological glimpse into the mind of a serious evangelical student, Jo, coming of age in the 1940s. She spends most of the book mentally tormented due to not living up to the demands of her faith. In fact, at times, she's on the verge of losing her mind. I related to Jo and wanted to see where the author took things. Is Ms. Nelson a believer? Does she buy into all that with which she seems so intimately acquainted? If not, what has she

left behind? What's the point of the book? I took away two insights and the last quarter century has only underscored their value:
1. "It's a mistake to let a discussion of God be reduced simply to rational argument. Making faith intellectually respectable can be a trap. We must always come back to mystery…" Chapter eight, "Finding God," and Appendix 1, "For the Road," are very much in synch with this insight.
2. "Loving, we tremble on the brink of disaster. But to pull back—that was extinction." This fascinating quote brings us back to the topic at hand.

Not Pulling Back

Growing up, I decorated my room with posters, especially those with wildlife or motivational themes. They've all long since been taken down, all that is, except one and I laminated it. It's a picture of gymnast Nadia Comaneci on a balance beam—the gymnast I had watched, alongside my father, get perfect 10s in the 1976 Olympics. She is gracefully poised and the muscles on her legs are pronounced. Steel comes to mind. Over her picture are the words, "Don't pray for an easy life; pray to be a strong person." This prayer is a significant part of who I am as my name, Greg, means "guardian" or "watchful one." It's hard to watch and guard in isolation, however, and, whether I like it or not, God's will always involves courage and people. Like Jim Croce's lyric from chapter five, "I've got a name" but it's hard to live it out if you keep pulling back.

Although it was like going back into the belly of the beast, I returned to Berachah in 1990—now trying to rebrand itself as Calvary. Why would I go back to a place that had done so much damage to my family and others?

There were several reasons but it began with an intersection of opportunity and need. Having recently graduated from Philadelphia Biblical University (now Cairn) in Langhorne, Pennsylvania, I was looking for a part-time ministry position to supplement my carpentry work. At twenty-four, I already had a reputation as one of the most skilled carpenters in the area and had even started my own business. That's when I heard about Woody.

Woody was the new senior pastor of Calvary, Berachah rebranded, who had been hired to build something from the ash heap of the Janson's legacy. I don't remember exactly how we first met, but we hit it off, and he wanted someone to help who understood the challenges he was facing. Woody was an incredible optimist with a great sense of humor. He laid out a vision that affirmed my gifts, offering free housing and a part-time pastoral role.

It all seemed providential. The church had just purchased a six-bedroom Victorian farmhouse that needed significant renovations. With my skill, there was opportunity to do a lot of the work and fix it up in a way that was customized to our tastes. At the time, it seemed like a significant step up from the tiny, deteriorating mobile home we were renting.

Additionally, there was a part of me that wanted to go back to repair or heal the brokenness which I and others had experienced. Maybe God had comforted me in my pain so that I might comfort others?[3] Maybe I was uniquely qualified for "such a time as this?"[4]

It took a lot of courage to drive up to the property and walk through the doors of the church again. To walk down the concrete block halls of the basement and go into the various rooms. For some, it would have been like going through a little shop of horrors; for me, it was like returning to prison. Every person's "trauma trigger" is different. One former Berachite shared that his trigger was the red carpet in the halls and sanctuary. Upon returning and seeing it, memories of preaching that reeked with hell-fire threatened to overwhelm him and make him sick.

Again, for me, there were lots of ghosts. Many painful memories. But I understood what many still standing had been through, all victims in some way—including a few that had been the Jansons' chief enforcers, "yes-men," and perpetrators. Again,

---

[3] 2 Corinthians 1:4.
[4] Esther 4:14.

despite how, just seven years prior, many had shunned and spread rumors about my family and me, I still cared and I wanted to help.

Deciding to accept the position, I was hired as Assistant Pastor and then, shortly after, ordained as an independent Baptist minister. Most of my responsibilities included student ministries and music but, when the pastor was away, I would also preach. Shortly into my tenure, the senior pastor left on vacation, leaving me to hold down the fort.

May 1, 1991 is a day I'll never forget. I had just returned home from leading youth group and was starting to unwind when the phone rang. I answered to hear that three of my students had been in a car accident on their way home and, although the person calling didn't know the details, they thought it was serious. Not knowing what to expect, I quickly left for the hospital being assured that one of the deacons would be there to meet me.

I arrived to see two of the kids from youth group, a brother and sister—Nathan and Susanna, in the emergency ward covered with cuts and bruises. At that moment, their mom, Tina, was still trapped in the car and their other sister, Becky, was in a coma and being flown to a university hospital twenty minutes away. (Tragically, Tina would die before they were ever able to get her out of the vehicle. Becky would recover but remain in intensive care for months.) Then the father, Wayne, who had not been with them at the time of the accident arrived. Here I was, now just twenty-five, with the task of telling a man and his two children that they had just lost a wife and a mother. Throughout the painful process, we cried together and I'm grateful there was another church leader with me that night because I don't think I could have done it myself. I wondered if the night would ever end.

This would be a difficult Sunday to preach, funeral arrangements needed to be made, and nobody seemed to be able to locate the senior pastor. These were the days before cell phones and, although I was scheduled to preach and lead the services that Sunday, I wasn't sure I was up to the task. I had known Tina since we had first come to Berachah when I was seven. She became one of my mom's best friends and our families had been very close until we left. In fact, even in my return to what was now Calvary, I was still one of Tina's favorites and she was the only person left on the planet that I still allowed to call me "Greggie." As I reeled over the loss of someone who loved me so much—the closest person to me to ever die tragically—Sunday was coming, and I would need to bring comfort to a church full of hurting people. I struggled for three days over what passage to preach from and what to say, yet with a grave sense of responsibility to comfort God's people.

Emotionally exhausted, I continued to pray and work on the message, and then, Sunday came. I preached from Psalm 46, "God is our refuge and our strength, a very present help in trouble...." I shared with them what I had experienced in the struggle to prepare the sermon; that is, that God brings strength to his people. I meant it and they knew it. We connected and, due to this shared adversity, feeling my love for them, and God's anointing, they were riveted to every word. I don't believe the Senior Pastor could have done what God placed me there to do that week. In finishing the task, I was filled with a sense of peace and gratefulness that I had been allowed to speak for God. As a bonus, my only sister who had been running from God for five years—profoundly impacted by Tina's death, recommitted her life to Christ.

This entire week-long experience was a "baptism of fire" and was seminal to my vocational call to comfort, strengthen, and encourage the church. And it never would have happened if I had pulled back. Clearly, God had his hand on and was leading me. The picture of Nadia's steel muscles remains a symbol of an internal strength that only God can give. It's that river I mentioned earlier that runs through all of our stories and is ultimately connected to his throne.[5] In all this—including returning to the church that had hurt my family so deeply, I learned that sometimes love means simply choosing courage over comfort, being there in the toughest moments of life, pushing through pain and exhaustion—not abandoning your brothers and sisters but bringing them hope.

---

[5] Psalm 46:4a.

Shame-based versus Grace-based Churches

God's truth brings hope and with it comes freedom,[6] another gift of love I tried to leave with folks at Calvary. In 1990, a book came out called *Released from Shame* by Dr. Sandra Wilson. I was drawn to the title and immediately zeroed in on a chapter called "Released from Shame-based Concepts of God and Religion." Boy, did I resonate with that section. There were two, two-columned charts that were especially helpful. One contrasted "Shame-based vs. God-directed Service," and the other 'Shame-based vs. Grace-based Church Families." The hypocrisy of the Jansons' sexual and severe physical abuse aside, it was this second, simple, one-page chart that showed me Berachah's doctrinal error and ugliness more vividly that I had ever seen it before. Here are just two examples and these caused me to prioritize small groups in my ministry at Calvary:

- In shame-based churches like Berachah, attendance of church activities is used as the main indicator of a person's true spirituality. But this perspective is reductionistic, tends to ignore the presence (or lack, thereof) of the fruits of the Holy Spirit[7], and focuses on externals rather than the heart. In reality, Wilson points out, in grace-based churches "true spirituality is reflected in total lifestyle and is known only to God.[8]

- In shame-based churches, "small-group Bible studies are dangerous places because someone might get close enough to see behind my mask of perfection and know I have problems." In grace-based churches "small-group Bible studies are safe places to practice being maskless and to be with others who do the same. It's great to go where I don't have to hide my problems."[9]

Related to this topic of grace-based churches providing safe

---

[6] John 8:32.
[7] Gal. 5:22-23.
[8] Sandra D. Wilson, *Released from Shame* (Downers Grove, IL: IVP, 2002), 151.
[9] Ibid.

places to be real, I had a close college buddy call me several years ago on a Saturday night and he was clearly in distress. He, together with his wife and five children, had been preparing to go overseas to London as independent Baptist missionaries to plant a second church. Of note, they had returned to the states on furlough after successfully planting their first church in Australia. They were now poised to go on a new adventure—they had their tickets and everything. Then, just days before their departure, his wife left him. That was tragic enough for my friend but what I found most telling was this: Obviously there were issues and his wife felt overwhelmed and afraid, but why did she feel it necessary to leave so dramatically and act out so severely? And why was it that when my friend called me, he neither had nor wanted to confide in his pastor or any other trusted member in his church?

Why? Because there was no safe person to be real with, no context in the church they were part of for open, honest confession of sin or struggle.[10] They were part of a church and network, as I had been at Berachah, that taught them to hide their faults, act as spiritual as possible, and judge others who had problems. Ken Blue in his book *Healing Spiritual Abuse* gives three messages of unhealthy churches:

- There is no time for you to disclose your sin.
- There is no place to get ministry for your pain.
- There's no one to help shoulder your burden.[11]

I've learned in the years since Berachah that the best contexts to cultivate appropriate, open and honest confession are close friendships, marriages, families, pastoral or mentoring relationships, and small groups. These are all contexts where the necessary trust to make "a safe place" can be cultivated and enjoyed. One of the core values I now live by when it comes to church—a ministry priority that began at Calvary—is "Maturity requires mentoring and life-change often happens best in small groups." As Ken Blue notes again:

---

[10] James 5:13-16.
[11] Ken Blue, *Healing Spiritual Abuse*.

All churches do not have the human resources or the spiritual and psychological skills to meet every need. But providing a safe place to disclose needs and have them received is a central mandate of the church and the very least we can do.[12]

How God Uses Our Kids

In 1992, I left Calvary with my wife, Pam, and first-born, six-month-old son, Matthew, to attend seminary in Louisville, Kentucky and further prepare for full-time pastoral ministry. I also took another part-time associate job at an Evangelical Free Church. Early in my ministry there, one well-respected, elderly gentleman named Milliard said, "Greg, children will teach you things about love you never knew." Although I didn't understand all that he meant at the time, his statement has turned out to be one of the most profound truths ever said to me. I had learned about shame-based versus graced-based churches, but now I was about to take on the challenge of shame-based versus grace-based parenting.

Besides the joy of watching kids grow and doing fun things like Christmas, walks in the park, vacations at the beach, and even re-watching classic movies or TV again through their eyes, I learned parenting also comes with many difficulties. The amount of sacrifice, of death to self, in order to serve and love well astounded me. Milliard, the dear saint, had tried to prep me for it. But in the experience of putting my kids' needs first, I finally understood what he meant. Finding a way to give them what they needed when I had no physical strength or financial resources left. Consistently putting your desires second or last for a time because their needs require it. Trying to comfort a sick, handicapped, or distressed child in the middle of the night when you're exhausted. Or when you need to go see what's wrong with your teenager or follow-up on some discipline you've given them, and you can't get yourself up off the couch emotionally or physically. In these times, love requires initiative, effort, pulling from some internal reservoir, giving—yes,

---

[12] Ibid.

giving even when it hurts.

"Trembling on the Brink of Disaster"

Returning to Shirley Nelson's provocative quote from *The Last Year of War,* let's focus on the first sentence in bold: "Loving, we tremble on the brink of disaster. But to pull back—that was extinction." We touched on this trembling and disaster—this precariousness—above in talking about sacrificing till it hurts for our children. And in the circle of life, many of us get to do this again in caring for an aging parent. But love can also be dangerous.

Singer/songwriter Wayne Watson captures this dilemma, in his song "Untouched By Human Hands," based on his reflections on an odd promise from the longer ending of Mark:[13] "they will pick up serpents with their hands, and if they drink any deadly poison, it will not hurt them" (18a). Watson asks, "Was his vision so spectacularly seen? Some exhibition, some display? Or a reminder as I live and breathe to reach out and not be afraid?" He then belts out in the chorus: "I try to be a godly man. I try to walk in the steps of Jesus. I disobey the Lord's command when I walk through this journey untouched by human hands."[14]

Whether Mark 16:18a was originally part of holy Scripture or not, Watson's point is clear: in "loving," we risk rejection, betrayal, and abuse. There's just no way around it. We learn that sometimes love means acceptance when we don't agree with someone's choices. When our kids or parents choose a girlfriend, boyfriend, or life partner who is less than we would prefer, often we have to learn to love who they bring home. And that can get messy if children are involved, we don't share the same values, or boundaries aren't respected. What does love look like in these instances? Often there are no easy answers.

In cases where I've had family members that seemed impossible to love, this wisdom from Mother Teresa has helped:

---

[13] Mark is the oldest gospel and has several alternate endings. The longer ending, 16:9-20, is not included in some of the earliest manuscripts.
[14] Wayne Watson, *The Fine Line* (Sony Records, 1992).

People are often unreasonable, irrational, and self-centered. Forgive them anyway.

If you are kind, people may accuse you of selfish, ulterior motives. Be kind anyway.

If you are successful, you will win some unfaithful friends and some genuine enemies. Succeed anyway.

If you are honest and sincere people may deceive you. Be honest and sincere anyway.

What you spend years creating, others could destroy overnight. Create anyway.

If you find serenity and happiness, some may be jealous. Be happy anyway.

The good you do today, will often be forgotten. Do good anyway.

Give the best you have, and it will never be enough. Give your best anyway.

In the final analysis, it is between you and God. It was never between you and them anyway.[15]

Her counsel helped me attach my actions to the higher priority of loving God. By focusing my affections on Him, it became easier to show love to those who otherwise seemed unloveable. I've had to qualify this counsel in some instances, however, with Jesus's words not to "cast your pearls before swine." Jesus wasn't calling people pigs but saying, "Don't give precious treasures to people who don't appreciate them."

I've learned that sometimes love means letting go. Especially when it's revealed over time that a person doesn't want what you have, is hurting other primary individuals you are called to love, or is keeping you from needed growth or living as God has called you to live. Again, these are not easy scenarios and can be precarious even to think through.

But choice is the gift of adulthood and we need to respect that in others, even those with whom we disagree. We also need to remember that this gift of choice is our gift and responsibility too.

---

[15] http://prayerfoundation.org/mother_teresa_do_it_anyway.htm

Sometimes we need to make a hard choice to end a relationship that's destructive to us or our family.[16] In one instance, my wife, Pam, and I had to cut ourselves off from family involved in dangerous and destructive habits. In another instance, we had to end a long-term toxic friendship. Indeed, some of these decisions can be so painful it's like losing a limb. We understand why some might pull back, but risk and vulnerability are included in the call to love. Without the necessary suffering that goes with this territory,[17] we can't grow in wisdom, and greater God and self-awareness. How do you learn about God's long-suffering and mercy—even his tough love—if you have never had to give or experience these yourself?

Finding Ourselves

And that is a lot of what learning to love is all about: learning to feel the father heart of God, learning to be at home in his love. John, the closest friend and disciple to Jesus while he was on earth, said it best: "So we have *come to know and to believe* the love that God has for us. God is love, and whoever abides in love abides in God, and God abides in him."[18]

"God is love" is a phrase that's thrown around a lot in our day, yet one that's rarely given clarity. Although I've come to believe that love is at the heart of God—something John is stating clearly here, I don't believe it's just a gooey pile of sweets that we dole out to the masses. The late theologian Donald Bloesch helps us get it right:

> God in his essence *is* both love and holiness, and therefore it is of a holy love that we must speak when referring to divinity. God is love, but his love exists in tension with his holiness. There is both a kindness and a severity in God (Rom. 11:22), and neither must be emphasized to the

---

[16] The bestselling book, *Boundaries* by Henry Cloud and John Townsend does an excellent job describing the need for and ways to carry out this kind of tough love.
[17] Romans 5:3-5.
[18] 1 John 4:16, ESV.

detriment of the other. God's steadfast love endures forever (Psa. 136:1; 138:8), but it endures as a consuming fire.[19]

Berachah distorted so much of my view of God. Movies like *The Burning Hell* made me think God was more wrath than love, and then, detoxing from that, I spent another thirty-five years believing love and wrath were both attributes of God. In viewing John's statement above that "God is love," I stood with good-hearted teachers that said things like "certainly love is *a* very important attribute of God"[20] but were uncomfortable saying plainly that the essence of God is "holy love."

It has only been recently through teachers like N.T. Wright that I've come to understand that God's wrath, properly understood, is not another one of his attributes alongside love but "an aspect of his love."[21] It's because God loves people with "a steady, unquenchable passion"[22] that he hated the Holocaust, Sandy Hook, 911, and all mass killings. It's because of his love that he hates racism, sex trafficking, and all forms of abuse. It's because of his love that he hated all the shame, distorted views of sex, and heinous crimes against children at Berachah. It's because of his love that he hates all the "wounds time will not wash clean" in your life too. Wright reminds us that "if God is not wrathful against these things, he is not loving… And it is his love, determining to deal with that nasty, insidious, vicious, soul-destroying evil, that causes him to send his only, special son."[23]

Ultimately, we "find ourselves again" by coming to know and believe, more and more, that God loves us.[24] And a huge part of how we do that is through experience—learning to love. Being an engaged son, daughter, parent, grandparent, spouse, aunt, uncle, cousin, friend, fellow-human teaches us that love is so much more

---

[19] Donald Bloesch, *Essentials in Evangelical Theology* (Peabody, MA: Hendrickson, 2006), 32.
[20] https://www.patheos.com/blogs/randyalcorn/2018/03/love-is-not-god/
[21] N.T. Wright, *Lent for Everyone: Mark, Year B* (Louisville, KY: Westminster John Knox Press, 2012), 85.
[22] Ibid., 85.
[23] Ibid., 86.
[24] Again, 1 John 4:16.

than words, mere sentiments, and Hallmark platitudes totally detached from a heart to actually help. If you choose to put your head in the game, to pursue love, to give of yourself to others—to not pull back—you'll find it's also the path to greater healing and joy.

Yes, experiences like Berachah distort and destroy, and it's important to unpack and try to understand them (more on that in chapter nine). Thankfully, God's holy love resuscitates and restores. Be assured, he is good and wants to be known:

> "And it is impossible to please God without faith. Anyone who wants to come to him must believe that God exists and that he rewards those who sincerely seek him."[25]

---

[25] Hebrews 11:6, NLT.

CHAPTER EIGHT: FINDING GOD

Religion is dangerous because it allows human beings who don't have all the answers to think that they do.[1]
—Bill Maher

I have a lot of sympathy for Maher's perspective above or books like *Unfollow: Loving and Leaving Westboro Baptist Church* by Megan Phelps-Roper. And, in reading my story, I'm sure you understand why. As I told you earlier, I've had a love-hate relationship with the church for much of my life. Yes, I'm a religious person but I'm certainly not one with all the answers. My primary experience of God has been through music and nature, fatherhood, marriage, Scripture, and the cross. Regarding the natural world, I agree with C.S. Lewis who said:

> If we used [nature] as our only clue [to the existence of God], then I think we should have to conclude that He was a great artist (for the universe is a very beautiful place), but also that He is quite merciless and no friend to man (for the universe is a very dangerous and terrifying place).[2]

Why I Believe in a Loving Creator

For me, nature points to a Great Artist. Moreover, the beauty of human love, seen especially in a healthy family, points to a *loving* Creator. There we see beauty in the emotional and sexual union

---

[1] https://www.brainyquote.com/quotes/bill_maher_629355
[2] C.S. Lewis, *Mere Christianity* (New York: Touchstone, 1996), 37.

within marriage, and experience deep trust and interdependency between spouses, parents, and children. Interestingly, even when we *don't* see these things and experience brokenness in our relationships with our parents, spouse, or children, we retain an awareness of what things could be or should be.

Fatherhood especially has provided me with powerful evidence of a loving Creator who, in Christianity, reveals Himself as "Our Father." I remember traveling back down south to our home at Southern Seminary in Louisville, Kentucky in 1993. Our family was returning from a week of visiting our extended families back in southern New Jersey. We stopped for dinner, and I was sitting across from my oldest son, Matthew Gregory, at McDonald's. At the time, he was two years old, and I had just settled him on the orange plastic bench he was using as a jungle gym. As I helped him get more fries, he looked up, full of wonder and dependence, and said, "I love you, Daddy." It was the first time I had ever heard those words from him. My soul leapt, my heart smiled, and I immediately went over to the other side of the bench and, with tears, embraced him and said, "I love you too, bud."

Priceless experiences like this, as well as thirty-plus years of intimacy with my wife, Pam, have become indelible reasons of the heart—real evidences at the core of my being—for the existence of a loving creator.

And, although I'll touch briefly on various "divine" sources of revelation below, what the Bible reveals about God as "Our Father" rings true with my experience as a "Dad" and now—as a new grandfather!—"Papa." Again, "The fear of the LORD"[3] may be the beginning of wisdom, but it's not God's endgame. He never intended fear to be used as a primary pastoral tool. In fact, fear in the sense of apprehension, terror, or dread stands in the way of getting to know the heart of God. The apostle John, arguably Jesus' closest friend on earth, said that clearly:

> So we have come to know and to believe the love that God has for us. God is love, and whoever abides in love abides

---

[3] Proverbs 1:7, ESV.

in God, and God abides in him. By this is love perfected with us, so that we may have confidence for the day of judgment, because as he is so also are we in this world. There is no fear in love, but perfect love casts out fear. For fear has to do with punishment, and whoever fears has not been perfected in love.[4]

Veteran pastor and youth worker Chap Clark illustrates John's point well with his story of a young father and his three-year-old son:

Every day the father would come home after work and go through the same routine: walk into the kitchen, pour a glass of milk, grab a couple of cookies, and walk back into the living room to unwind while watching the evening news.

One night the father came home a little late, and as he walked in the door he noticed his three-year-old hurrying toward the kitchen. The father, sensing something was up, hesitated.

Dragging a chair, the little boy rushed over to the kitchen counter, climbed up, reached into the cupboard, and grabbed a glass—knocking over two in the process. Then he grabbed two cookies from the cookie jar (one fell on the floor), climbed down off the counter, and ran to the refrigerator. As he pulled out the jug of milk, it slipped out of his hands, landing on the floor and spilling some. Undaunted, the boy poured some of the remaining milk into the glass and set the carton back down on the floor. By now, the kitchen looked like a tornado had struck! The cupboard was open, the refrigerator door was open, and cookie crumbs and milk were all over the floor.

Any other night, the boy might have been disciplined for all the rules he had broken. But, as the father watched his son run down the hall with the glass of milk and cookie, he realized what love was in the boy's heart—and threw his arms around his son and said, "Thank you, son, for that wonderful gift!"

Too many of us view God as a stern father standing at the end of the hallway yelling, "You got cookie crumbs all over the floor!

---

[4] 1 John 4:16-18, ESV.

You left the cabinet door open! You spilled the milk! Get that refrigerator door closed!" But God isn't like that. Instead He throws His arms around us and says, "Thank you for that wonderful gift!"[5]

And so, to recap, nature leads me to God the amazing artist, and fatherhood and marriage reveal a God of relationship and goodness. From there, I reason that a loving Creator would not leave us without answers to our most challenging questions:

- Origin: Where did we come from?
- Meaning: What are we here for?
- Morality: What is good and what is evil?
- Destiny: Is there an afterlife and, if so, what will it be like?[6]

Why I'm a Christian

The question becomes, then, *where did a loving God give us answers to the questions above?* We could start with the five major world religions but which one?[7] Certainly answering these questions well is far beyond the scope of this project.[8] For me, however, the deciding factor was the evidence for the resurrection of Christ. What precipitated my in-depth study of this topic, however, was a serious crisis of faith. And believe it or not, it came in 1994 while I was at Southern Seminary in Louisville, immersed in discussions and study of God and the Bible.

---

[5] I've adapted this story from Chap Clarke's story as found in Mike Yaconelli & Jim Burns, *High School Ministry* (Grand Rapids, MI: Zondervan, 1986), 34.

[6] Although I cannot now locate the exact source, I first heard the information bulleted here in a lecture and Q&A that Ravi Zacharias did at Harvard University.

[7] The five major religions of the world are Judaism, Christianity, Hinduism, Buddhism, and Islam. Only three of them—Judaism, Christianity, and Islam—make claims to a universal, clear source(s) of authority; that is, the kind that answers our most challenging questions. Interestingly, these same three all claim allegiance to the God of Abraham, Isaac, and Jacob.

[8] The books I've found the most helpful or recommend in answering these questions well are Dr. Ravi Zacharias' Great Conversations series that include: *The Lotus and the Cross: Jesus Talks with Buddha*, *New Birth or Rebirth?: Jesus Talks with Krishna*. Also, *Engaging with Jewish People: Understanding Their World, Sharing Good News* by Randy Newman and *Seeking Allah, Finding Jesus: A Devout Muslim Encounters Christianity* by Nabeel Qureshi and Lee Strobel.

One day, as I wandered the nearby campus of Westminster Presbyterian Seminary, a solitary PCUSA school with several attractive stone buildings, I even seriously questioned the existence of God. As Kansas said in their song "Chasing Shadows in the Night": "All of us—we are an audience looking for evidence to help it all make sense." But as I walked, I reasoned, "How can we—how could I—be sure of anything... really? Maybe I was just spending a lot of time and money deluding myself, and religion really was just some kind of "wish fulfillment," or as Karl Marx said, "the opiate of the people."

Besides being exhausted due to the pace I was keeping, working ninety hours most weeks, this "dark night of the soul" was triggered by the death of my grandmother and being asked to do her memorial service. This grandmother was not my mom's mom who I talked so much about in chapter one, but my dad's mom.

They had asked me to do the service because I had been close to her in her later years. As a teenager, I had spent many lazy, breezy, summer days just talking next to her as we enjoyed a glass of tea on her green porch swing. We had also spent hours, together with my grandfather, in that same space playing pinochle or scrabble.

But the other reason I was asked to do the service was due to family politics. When my agnostic grandfather died on November 9th, 1988, the one who had taught me to think and play chess, a decision was made to have a pastor, who didn't even know my grandfather, give a hellfire and brimstone sermon at his memorial service. This didn't go over well, especially with the non-religious members of my family who saw it as a power play, as well as a slap in the face to a man who had spent most of his life contemptuous of religion.

Moreover, contrary to what I can only assume the presiding pastor desired, the service certainly didn't draw anyone closer to God; rather, it created a rift in our family that lasted for several years. When my grandmother died on February 22nd, 1994, I was in seminary studying to be a pastor. Despite my religious views, thankfully, I had a reputation in my extended family for treating others with gentleness and respect. Again, because I had also been close to my grandmother, I was the logical choice. Not only would my leading the service mitigate any risk of the rift getting worse, perhaps it could even bring healing to it.

Given this possibility, I was especially concerned that my demeanor and tone were loving, gracious, and empathetic, drawing my family to the message of Christ, not further away from it. And yet, as mentioned above, the request to do the service came at a time when I was exhausted and already wrestling with nagging questions about God's silence related to suffering, and especially the Christian teaching related to hell. It is one thing to be raised in, discuss, and study these things. It is quite another to stand up and preach about them with "Billy Graham conviction." As I prepared, I brought my doubts and apprehensions to God in prayer. Seeking answers in his Word, I found in Paul's first letter to the Corinthian church, the fifteenth chapter, a solid case for the reality of the resurrection.[9]

Paul's first and main argument centers on the historicity of the Christian faith and centers on the eyewitnesses that saw the resurrected Christ (verses 5–8). An appearance to Peter, then to the twelve disciples. Later Jesus showed himself to more than five hundred at one time. To us, two thousand years removed, we not only have the record of Paul's testimony given here, but also that contained in the gospel writings of Matthew, Mark, Luke, and John. John Stott notes that:

> An investigation of the ten appearances reveals an almost studied variety in the circumstances of person, place and mood in which they occurred. He was seen by individuals alone (Mary Magdalene, Peter, and James), by small groups and by more than 500 people together. He appeared in the garden of the tomb, near Jerusalem, in the upper room, on the road to Emmaus, by the lake of Galilee, on a Galilee mountain and on

---

[9] I'm defining resurrection here as the transformation of the body into an existence in which we have no experience.

the Mount of Olives.[10]

Paul's account in 1 Corinthians 15 was written 15–20 years after the resurrection. The idea was if anyone had doubts about the certainty of the event they could go ask around. This would certainly have served as incontrovertible evidence to readers at the time of Paul's writing.

Another powerful argument Paul makes in 1 Corinthians 15 is how the natural world supports the concept of resurrection. Almost without exception, denials of Jesus resurrection are not based on specific critiques of the historical accounts in the gospels, but rest solely on the contention that resurrection itself is not possible. For example, many say something like this: "I don't know why the disciples thought Jesus rose from the dead, but it seems to me that any explanation is better than the one which assumes he actually rose from the dead." Here's how Paul answers this objection:

- The resurrection is truly miraculous but is it any more miraculous than the birthing process? (45–49)
- Take a seed for instance (36), "what you sow does not come to life unless it dies." Right there in the simplicity of a garden seed is the phenomenon of life being brought about in death.
- Look at "the variety of bodies" around you (39–44). Notice that your flesh is different than the flesh of animals, birds or fish. Now look up, see the moon, stars, and sun. The beauty of the heavens is a different kind than what we see on earth. Is it really so unreasonable to imagine a heavenly existence that is imperishable, glorious, and powerful?

Besides the evidence from history and nature, the argument Paul gives that strengthened my faith the most is the one in which he plays devil's advocate. In 1 Corinthians 15, he says Christian belief in the afterlife is both truthful and credible because the alternative brings no hope and is illogical. Paul essentially says, "Try this on for size. See how plausible it feels. Here are a few realities

---

[10] John R. W. Stott, *Basic Christianity* (Grand Rapids: Eerdmans, 1978), 57.

you need to face if there is no resurrection from the dead:"
- Christ never rose from the dead. (13)
- Christian preaching amounts to nothing. (14)
- If you're a Christian, your belief system is devoid of truth. It is fruitless—without effect, empty, imaginary, and unfounded. (14,17)
- Paul and billions of others of like faith have misrepresented or are misrepresenting God. (15)
- Humanity is still under the control and penalty of sin. (17)
- Those who have died as Christians are lost. (18)
- All of us face the miserable and pitiful fact that we have no hope beyond this life. Eugene Peterson, in *The Message*, puts it this way: "If all we get out of Christ is a little inspiration for a few short years, we're a pretty sorry lot." (19)
- The idea of baptism for the dead (whatever this practice was) is meaningless. (19)
- We should all "eat, drink, and be merry" with no concern for eternity. (32) And finally, one of the greatest challenges...
- We must come up with some better explanation for why Paul continually risked his life for a lie. (32)

In all, it's not a pretty picture, again, both in how it feels and also in its logic. As Josh McDowell observed, "Nobody knowingly and willingly dies for a lie."

Today, I'm still amazed at how powerful Paul's defense of the resurrection is. Although many fine books have been written,[11] 1 Corinthians 15 is still one of the strongest cases for the resurrection of Jesus Christ and the credibility of the Christian faith. Paul shows how Christ's resurrection is historically, scripturally, logically, and naturally supported. More importantly, he shows what's at stake if

---

[11] Three of my favorites are *Surprised by Hope* by N.T. Wright (especially chapter four), *Loving God* by Chuck Colson (chapter six), and *The Case for Christ* by Lee Strobel (chapters 11-14).

it never happened, and how the fact that it did infuses the world with hope!

Although a reasonable faith is very important to me, I have not relied on my intellect alone to answer these questions. Working as a carpenter has taught me well the truth spoken by the great theologian, Clint Eastwood: "A man's got to know his limitations." Okay, maybe Clint isn't a theologian, but his words underscore the sheer folly of the idea that humans can figure things out without any help from God. In other words, experiencing our profound limitations drives us to seek answers outside ourselves.

Thomas Merton's prayer captures my heart well:

> My Lord God, I have no idea where I am going. I do not see the road ahead of me. I cannot know for certain where it will end. Nor do I really know myself and the fact that I think that I am following your will does not mean that I am actually doing so. But I believe the desire to please you does in fact please you. And I hope that I have that desire in all that I am doing. I hope that I will never do anything apart from that desire. And I know that if I do this you will lead me by the right road, though I may know nothing about it. Therefore I will trust you always though I may seem to be lost and in the shadow of death. I will not fear, for you are ever with me, and you will never leave me to face my perils alone.[12]

Although many will desire more exclusive content about Christ, Merton's prayer is honest about our limitations, capacity for self-deception, and need to throw ourselves wholly on the mercy of God. Even though I've done my fair share of study, it's honestly an unseen hand that's led me to a place of serenity and seeing Christianity and the Bible as God's answers to the questions that trouble us most. But what ultimately leads a person to see Jesus as the only way to God, and the Bible as God's Word? It's certainly beyond our capacity here to answer these questions well, and each

---

[12]Thomas Merton, *Thomas Merton: Spiritual Master*, (Paulist: Mahwah), 243.

person's journey to Christ is different.[13] There may be many roads to Jesus even if there is only one way to God.[14] As a Christian minister, I've come to see the death, burial, and resurrection of Christ as the center of Christianity, further evidence of a loving God, and the gateway at the end of "the many roads to Jesus."

What the Apostle Paul said 2000 years ago to a group of spiritual seekers rings true to what I've observed and experienced: "… that they should seek God, and perhaps feel their way toward him and find him. Yet he is actually not far from each one of us, for, 'In him we live and move and have our being.'"[15] I don't believe, however, anyone will ever "feel their way" toward God and "find him" without God first opening his or her eyes, revealing truth, and drawing that person to embrace Christ.[16] This is consistent with what Jesus taught in the gospels in recounting Peter's famous confession: "You are the Christ, the son of the living God."[17] When Peter said this, Jesus was quick to point out that God was responsible for Peter's revelation, not human agency: "Blessed are you…for flesh and blood has not revealed this to you, but my Father who is in heaven."[18]

If we are to have an "aha" moment like Peter, God must turn the light on. Only he can shatter our darkness and change our desires. If he does not both initiate and complete the work for this to happen, we will never "find him." When it comes to faith, grace is essential. I agree with Bono on this:

> You see, at the center of all religions is the idea of Karma. You know, what you put out comes back to you: an eye for an eye, a tooth for a tooth, or in physics—in physical laws—every action is met by an equal or an opposite one. It's clear

---

[13] The resources that have helped me the most in answering these questions include *Mere Christianity* by C.S. Lewis, *The Unknown God* by Alister McGrath, *The Prodigal God* by Tim Keller, and *Scripture and the Authority of God* by N.T. Wright.
[14] John 14:6.
[15] Acts 17:27-28.
[16] John 6:44a.
[17] Matthew 16:16, ESV.
[18] Matthew 16:17, ESV.

to me that Karma is at the very heart of the universe. I'm absolutely sure of it. And yet, along comes this idea called Grace to upend all that 'as you reap, so you will sow' stuff. Grace defies reason and logic. Love interrupts, if you like, the consequences of your actions, which in my case is very good news indeed, because I've done a lot of stupid stuff... I'd be in big trouble if Karma was going to finally be my judge. I'd be in deep shit. It doesn't excuse my mistakes, but I'm holding out for Grace. I'm holding out that Jesus took my sins onto the Cross, because I know who I am, and I hope I don't have to depend on my own religiosity.[19]

In the mysterious "game" of life, with Grace as the catalyst, I've pushed all my chips representing all I am and all I'm not in front of God. I'm all in and everything is on Jesus. Although I have a heart that's prone to wander and a propensity, like the Apostle Peter, to deny Jesus with my words and actions, I resonate with his famous statement to Jesus in John 6:68: "…Lord, to whom would we go? You alone have the words that give eternal life. We believe them, and we know you are the Holy One of God." (NLT)

Yes, I'm a disciple of Jesus Christ. I stand with Peter and echo this apt description of what all disciples mean when they embrace his great words above:

> They know that the presence that has called them is dependable and that while they may be insecure, volatile, and easily capable of betrayal, forgetting and running away, what they confront in the person they call Rabbi and Master is one who will *not* go away.[20]

Still Plenty of Questions

Now, even though I've found answers in the Christian faith, I still live with many questions. Exactly how, why, and when God does what he does or allows what he allows are mysteries we'll never

---

[19] http://www.christianitytoday.com/ct/2005/augustweb-only/bono-0805.html
[20] Rowan Williams, *Being Disciples* (Grand Rapids, MI: Eerdmans, 2016), 26.

comprehend on this side of Heaven.[21] That's why, as I've gotten older—and to do justice to the thoughts that keep us up at night—I like to talk about theology as "mystery discerning" rather than "problem-solving." Richard Mouw, in his book *Adventures in Evangelical Civility*, quotes Catholic theologian Thomas Weinandy, who explains that "to solve a problem… is to make our puzzles go away, and that is not the kind of resolution that we ought to expect as a matter of course in theological exploration. But we can hope to succeed in knowing 'more precisely and clearly what the mystery is.'"[22] As Joni Eareckson Tada—someone well acquainted with suffering—said in her devotional, *Secret Strength*, "God is a water tower and we have Dixie cups."[23]

Although I have a high view of Scripture, I believe we need church tradition to help us understand the Bible correctly. And, although, I've found a home in Presbyterianism, I identify most with those that desire a kinder, gentler Calvinism. I want to worship in a community that celebrates "beautiful orthodoxy" from all three branches of Christianity,[24] healthy homes, the virtue of civility, racial and ethnic diversity, and a high esteem for scientific and literary accomplishments.

I agree with many, including atheists and agnostics, that see the problem of pain as the greatest barrier to the Christian faith. How could a good and all-powerful God allow unjust suffering? Why is God so silent? Do our sufferings really matter to the Almighty?

In 1993, I saw *Schindler's List*. Spielberg vividly portrayed the horrors of the Holocaust in a way that changed me forever. I walked out of the theater resolved to always give proper respect to the problem of pain. Today, whether I talk with my brother-in-law and am reminded of my sister's traumatic brain injury and the devastation it has brought to her family, or watch Martin Scorsese's *Silence* with my son, that resolve and respect remain.

---

[21] Isaiah 55:8.
[22] Richard J. Mouw, *Adventures in Evangelical Civility* (Grand Rapids, MI: Brazos Press, 2016), 16.
[23] Joni Eareckson Tada, *Secret Strength* (Portland, OR: Multnomah, 1988), 161.
[24] That is, the Roman Catholic, Protestant, and Orthodox Churches.

Hope and the Father Heart of God

As one who's suffered from religious abuse, I've come to take great Hope in God's promises to not waste pain in the lives of those who love Him. He works even through the ugliest trials, redeeming and shaping them into something that conforms to his good purposes:

- "And we know that God causes all things to work together for good to those who love God, to those who are called according to His purpose."[25]
- "Praise be to the God and Father of our Lord Jesus Christ, the Father of compassion and the God of all comfort, who comforts us in all our troubles, so that we can comfort those in any trouble with the comfort we ourselves receive from God."[26]

Viewed through the lens of these promises, I'm thankful that despite the deceit and malformation of my early adolescent and teenage church experience, I heard the gospel—that good news that sins are forgiven by the death, burial, and resurrection of the Son.[27] Especially as a teenager and young adult, I struggled with my ability to discern—or even understand the importance of having—a specific point in time that I personally responded to or "accepted" the gospel. My difficulty in this area came from trying to combine my normal, unexciting, and gradual growth in belief—in a seriously dysfunctional church environment—with the dramatic change reflected in many conversion stories. It also came because I was part of a tradition that, contrary to Jesus and Paul, constantly emphasized a personal sign-post; that is, the need to know the specific date and time when you became a Christian.

In Scripture, most don't have a knock-you-off-your-horse story like the apostle Paul. What Jesus and especially Paul *do* consistently emphasize, however, is that Christianity is the

---

[25] Romans 8:28, NASB. Regrettably, this is one of the most misunderstood and misapplied verse in the Bible and I'll say more about this in the conclusion.
[26] 2 Corinthians 1:3-4, NIV.
[27] 1 Corinthians 15:1-4.

justification of the ungodly.[28] In Paul's writings, justification is "an act of God's free grace, where he pardons all our sins, and accepts us as righteous in His sight, only for the righteousness of Christ imputed to us, and received by faith alone."[29]

In other words, Christianity is trusting in the sacrifice of Christ to make you right with God. It is not mere intellectual assent but a commitment of your whole person to Christ. As the hymn says, "my Hope is built on nothing less than Jesus' blood and righteousness!" For all of us—whatever tradition we're in *or not in*—it's not about the Mass, or the bread and wine, or baptism, or good doctrine, or prayers honoring saints, or confession, or Tim Keller preaching, or Mother Teresa good works. All those things, at their very best, point to or are directed at Christ. When any of them become ends in and of themselves, they are idols that keep us from God. We find God by putting on the Lord Jesus Christ. By standing in the perfect righteousness of His sacrifice on the cross. It's faith and trust in Christ alone that brings peace with and pleases God. We stand before God void of righteousness and cry, "God, be merciful to me, a sinner." (Luke 18:13b) That's the heart of a true Christian.

These verses say it plainly and have led me to the Father's heart—a place where I have found healing and rest:

- "Jesus said to him, I am the way, the truth, and the life. No one comes to the Father except through me."[30]
- "And without faith it is impossible to please him, for whoever would draw near to God must believe that he exists and that he rewards those who seek him."[31]
- "For it is by grace you have been saved, through faith—and this is not from yourselves, it is the gift of God—not by works, so that no one can boast."[32]

---

[28] Romans 3:28, 4:1-8, 5:1; Galatians 3:6-9.
[29] Westminster Shorter Catechism.
[30] John 14:6, ESV.
[31] Hebrews 11:6, ESV.
[32] Ephesians 2:8-9, NIV.

CHAPTER NINE: WHY IT HAPPENED

One of the places evil people are most likely to be found is within the church. What better way to conceal one's evil from oneself, as well as from others, than to be a deacon or some other highly visible form of Christian within our culture? . . . . I do not mean to imply that the evil are anything other than a small minority among the religious or that the religious motives of most people are in any way spurious. I mean only that evil people tend to gravitate toward piety for the disguise and concealment it can offer them.[1]
—M. Scott Peck, M.D

Looking back, I view my family's decade-long shame-based, legalistic church experience as extremely soul-killing. Further, I hold it partially responsible for my parents' divorce after twenty-six years of marriage. Why did all this happen? Although I don't want to be reductionistic or oversimplify life's complexities, I do want to provide some useful insights. Given this aim, here are seven main reasons, along with the most important lessons I've learned, which I hope will enhance your life.

Loss of Spiritual Support

I mentioned in chapter one, in the context of discussing the powerful double helix of faith and family, that my mom's parents brought a spiritual strength and stability to our family just by their proximity. When they left the area, a healthy spiritual influence was

---

[1] M. Scott Peck, *People of the Lie: The Hope of Healing Human Evil* (New York: Simon & Schuster, 1983), 76-77.

lost. I also explained that this was *one of the factors* that contributed to my mom's lack of spiritual support and vulnerability to bad religion. I say *one of the factors* because there were others and several are worth mentioning in this chapter.

Although there are spiritual hazards to ignoring the value of geographic proximity in passing on the faith, separation and detachment are often inescapable. We're not an agrarian society and, increasingly, there are fewer and fewer small towns. Yes, we're more globally connected and saturated with information, but we're also more fragmented, transient, isolated, and lonely. Thankfully, welcoming churches can also provide new homes and new families. In all scenarios, robust discipleship, however, is essential. Only this can fortify families and individuals against error and whatever losses or separations the future brings.

Take-away #1: Where possible, geographic closeness to healthy family is a gift and goal worth pursuing. Where it's not, emotional proximity is still possible. Determine to stay connected heart-to-heart, and make full use of technology that will help you do that.

Lack of Robust Discipleship

There was a lack of robust discipleship in my grandfather's pastoral ministry—my mom's formative church experience—that also contributed to her vulnerability. On Sundays in many churches, just like the one my grandfather cared for, there may be a beautiful and formative liturgy—even a focused homily, but use of a personal Bible in any form is unnecessary.

Congregants know little of its contents and, barring a possible Sunday School or confirmation class, there's insufficient training on how to handle the Bible correctly. One mom scornfully described the watered-down classes her own children experienced as "God loves you. Draw a tree." Churches like these do not build strong, mature, devoted disciples who easily think for themselves, discern error, and actively follow Christ. Instead they produce weak disciples who are vulnerable to the abuse and over-literalization of the Bible characteristic of fundamentalism[2] and many cults.[3] Further, these untrained Christians are susceptible to distorted views of God, sex, church government, end times, the place of suffering and rules, how to handle the Old Testament, the role and dignity of women, how God motivates us, the value of science (including psychology), and other issues.

Undeveloped, emotionally unhealthy disciples are vulnerable to leaders who manipulate and control using shame and fear—motivations that are regularly reinforced by hearing about a God who is constantly angry and likes to burn things. Rules become primary, not relationships. Fledgling believers are, again, bullied with fear and shame, learning little of higher motivations like grace, reward, or the joy of being a beloved, adopted part of God's family.[4]

That's definitely a part of my mom and our family's story, particularly the later deception by toxic leaders. But churches that are weak in discipleship also produce disengaged spectators—those who, as they enter adulthood, are more secular than Christian. Indeed, as we are now almost a quarter of the way into the twenty-first century, many have left the church altogether. Charles Taylor in his book *The Secular Age* describes our time as one where people are "haunted by the transcendent" and feel like "I don't believe in God, but I miss him." Taylor observes that even "believers are beset by doubt and doubters find themselves tempted by belief."[5]

Though the cultural water we swim in may be different than the early church or even my grandfather's time, when it comes to Christian discipleship, we share the same challenges. The writer of

---

[2] I'm using fundamentalism here to describe a rigid, isolated, and anti-intellectual expression of Christianity that's big on rules, taking the Bible literally with no sensitivity to its historical context or various genres, and viewing people who think or act differently as inferior. Fundamentalism produces disciples that are arrogant, don't listen, and could care less about civility (1 Pet. 3:15).

[3] There are thousands of horror stories of people using the Bible to justify abusive discipline, the mistreatment of women, apocalyptic craziness, and even genocide and covering over heinous crimes against children.

[4] John 1:12.

[5] James K. A. Smith, *How (Not) to Be Secular: Reading Charles Taylor* (Grand Rapids, MI: Errdmans, 2014), 4ff.

Hebrews put it like this:

> We have much to say about this, but it is hard to make it clear to you because you no longer try to understand. In fact, though by this time you ought to be teachers, you need someone to teach you the elementary truths of God's word all over again. You need milk, not solid food! Anyone who lives on milk, being still an infant, is not acquainted with the teaching about righteousness. But solid food is for the mature, who by constant use have trained themselves to distinguish good from evil.[6]

And it's further clarifying to connect this "solid food" and "constant use" to Dr. Luke's positive comments on the Berean's enthusiasm and diligence in studying Scripture:

> Now the Berean Jews were of more noble character than those in Thessalonica, for they received the message with great eagerness and examined the Scriptures every day to see if what Paul said was true.[7]

Commenting on the verse above, The *ESV Study Bible* notes:

> By commending this activity, Luke encourages this searching of the Scriptures as a pattern for all believers and also gives support to the doctrine of the clarity of Scripture, the idea that the Bible can be understood rightly, not only by scholars but also by ordinary people who read it eagerly and diligently, with conscious dependence on God for help.[8]

Looking at the Hebrews and the Acts passages together, we learn that biblical discipleship:

- **Consistently points to Christ**—In the Hebrews passage, the objective is "deeper understanding of fundamental truths… in the light of teaching about Jesus as Son of God

---

[6] Hebrews 5:11-14, NIV.
[7] Acts 17:11, NIV. Words in bold, mine.
[8] Crossway Bibles. (2008). The ESV Study Bible (p. 2121). Wheaton, IL: Crossway Bibles.

and high priest of the new covenant."⁹ In other words, they needed "some guidelines for interpreting the OT ('the oracles of God') from a Christian point of view."¹⁰ We see this is Acts as well, where the Bereans "studied their Old Testament with Paul to see if it pointed to Christ."¹¹ As Fleming Rutledge reminds us:

> The early Christians had no New Testament. Their single source for discovering the meaning of the strange death of their Lord was the Scriptures they had always known. Imagine the attention with which early Christian leaders searched every syllable of the Hebrew Bible, seeking to understand how the terrible death of the Son of God had been in the mind and plan of God all along.¹²

- **Grows people who, in time, are able to explain what they've learned**—This is implied in the phrase "by this time you ought to be teachers." The ability "to explain" is what's key here, not the mastery of some study Bible or even the ability to read. Most of us take our ability to read for granted; however, "only 12% of the people in the world could read and write in 1820."¹³ And the percentage was far lower for most of history.

- **Produces disciples who respond with faith and obedience**—this is the key idea behind the "constant use" of the Hebrews passage: they respond to what they hear. Additionally, the "teaching of righteousness" in Hebrews 5:13 is "teaching which can motivate them to righteousness

---

⁹ Peterson, D. G. (1994). Hebrews. In D. A. Carson, R. T. France, J. A. Motyer, & G. J. Wenham (Eds.), New Bible commentary: 21st century edition (4th ed., p. 1334). Leicester, England; Downers Grove, IL: Inter-Varsity Press.
¹⁰ Ibid.
¹¹ Polhill, J. B. (1998). Acts. In D. S. Dockery (Ed.), Holman concise Bible commentary (p. 525). Nashville, TN: Broadman & Holman Publishers.
¹² Fleming Rutledge, *The Crucifixion* (Grand Rapids: Eerdmans, 2015), 243.
¹³ https://ourworldindata.org/literacy .

(cf. 12:11)."[14]
- **Engages the heart and is associated with hunger for God**—We see this in the Bereans "eagerness."
- **Promotes open-minded, fair, and thoughtful engagement with scripture**—"Noble" translates "the Greek eugenēs, which originally meant "of noble birth" or "well born." The word was also applied to people who exhibited noble behavior, in that they were open-minded, fair, and thoughtful."[15]

As it relates to the local church or the double helix of faith and family, robust discipleship is about transforming babies into Bereans. The goal is to produce followers of Christ that are both well-learned and well-practiced.

Take-away #2: Build strong, devoted disciples who are constantly looking personally and pointing others to Christ, know how to handle the Bible correctly, can easily think for themselves and discern error, and actively live out their faith.

Devaluing the Role of Women

Berachah and even the church my parents went to after that did not understand the value of building into and empowering women to be strong, independent thinkers—the kind that are okay having a perspective or existence that is different or separate from a man's. And, in my grandfather's case, even as a Lutheran minister, it was more important to get my mom married off to a nice guy than it was to a nice guy who was also a Christian.

In a previous fellowship of churches, I was often asked to speak when a pastor was away. On one occasion, I asked my daughter to come up front and read the passage I was preaching on that morning before I spoke. To my surprise, a fellow pastor in our

---

[14] Peterson, D. G. (1994). Hebrews. In D. A. Carson, R. T. France, J. A. Motyer, & G. J. Wenham (Eds.), New Bible commentary: 21st century edition (4th ed., p. 1334). Leicester, England; Downers Grove, IL: Inter-Varsity Press.
[15] Crossway Bibles. (2008). The ESV Study Bible (p. 2121). Wheaton, IL: Crossway Bibles.

denomination wrote a letter questioning why we would let a woman stand behind the pulpit and lead the congregation in the Scripture reading. He felt this was a violation of 1 Timothy 2:12-13 and other passages.[16] I thought his position was ludicrous and hated the message he was sending to my daughter: Be quiet. Don't get too near holy things. Leave that to the men. Stay in your place.

This attitude toward girls and women is foreign to Jesus' ministry. In the gospels, "women were first at the cradle and last at the cross."[17] Jesus praised Mary for her "better choice:" sitting at his feet and learning like a disciple.[18] Not to mention, it was women that were sent out by Jesus as the first apologists of his resurrection.[19]

In my ministry, I agree with those who believe "it is a moral imperative in our time to combat child abuse, marginalization of women, and cruel masculine gods…"[20] I have no wish to contribute to what Dorothy Sayers, one of the first women to graduate from Oxford, called "a period when empty head and idle hands were qualities for which a man prized his woman and despised her."[21] Women were made for more than just being marriage "helpers," having babies, being pretty, and showing up.

In contrast to biblical times, women are now viewed as full persons that can vote and pursue many opportunities not afforded to them even a hundred years ago. (Remember, blacks were not viewed as full persons who could vote until 1870; for women, it was 1920!) The apostle Paul's command in 1 Timothy 2:11 to "Let a woman learn *in silence*…" can be used as a proof text to silence women or, more properly, as an encouragement that they should learn and grow: "Let a woman *learn*…." In the first century, "Women were less likely to be literate than men, were trained in philosophy far less often than men, were trained in rhetoric almost

---

[16] 1 Corinthians 11:1-16; 14:34-36.
[17] Dorothy L. Sayers, *Are Women Human?* (Grand Rapids: Eerdmans, 1971), 68.
[18] Luke 10:38-42.
[19] Matthew 28:10.
[20] Fleming Rutledge, *The Crucifixion* (Grand Rapids: Eerdmans, 2015), 261.
[21] Dorothy L. Sayers, *Are Women Human?* (Grand Rapids: Eerdmans, 1971), 63.

never, and in Judaism were far less likely to be educated in the law...the vast majority of rabbis would never accept a woman as a disciple."[22] It's important to see, however, that Paul's instruction in 1 Timothy 2:11 is both pastoral and—for his time—progressive. It is pastoral in that biblical teaching is guarded from those weak in Scripture. It is progressive in that women are encouraged to learn.

Take-away #3: Value women like Jesus did. Invest in and empower them to be strong, think independently, develop their full potential, and freely share their true thoughts and opinions.

Low Literacy

In southern New Jersey, the county I grew up in became the poorest in the state. In the area of literacy, for example, and the last I checked, only 13% of county residents have a bachelor's degree or higher. Further, the county ranked the lowest in New Jersey in school testing and high school completion rates. During the 70s, there were lots of clothing and glass factories and, therefore, lots of assembly line workers that functioned best with Captain Kirk-type leaders that told them what to think and do. Most were afraid of "the big city" (Philadelphia was our closest), and also afraid of the "secular humanism" that was permeating the culture. These conditions were ripe for a religious fundamentalism that plays on fears, encourages isolation, and insists on always taking the Bible literally.

And so, South Jersey's low literacy and lack of critical thinking are part of the story of why a ministry like Berachah's could thrive for a time. What's more, literacy, passivity, and the use of the mind are directly related to knowing and handling the Bible correctly or incorrectly. As an illustration of how lower literacy can make one vulnerable to bad or no religion, one dear father I knew went to his grave having read only one book in his life, a book about Greg Brady of *The Brady Bunch*. To this day, four of his five children are unchurched and show surprising susceptibility to error. They are not comfortable with reading, especially classic literature, so the

---

[22] See Craig Keener's insights in the *IVP Bible Background Commentary*, 611.

Bible is largely an unknown treasure that they think can only be interpreted with wooden literalism. They know nothing about the historical grammatical method of interpretation, Scripture's various literary genres, or how different parts of the Bible appeal to different parts of us. For example, they do not know how the psalms speak to our emotions, the letters of Paul to our minds, apocalyptic literature to our imagination, or the prophets to our will.

That's why we need to champion thinking moms and dads united in healthy marriages that will raise kids who seek out and lead spiritually healthy families, love the Bible, and know how to handle it correctly. Homes that prioritize reading—especially ones where parents snuggle with their children while reading to them—will form natural attachments and even safeguards against fear and passivity. For example, a daughter's self-esteem is best predicted by her father's physical affection. In fact, the Journal of the American Medical Association found that girls with doting fathers are more assertive.[23]

Moreover, the discipline and joy of reading is directly related to growing kids that are culturally literate and who appreciate the past, including classic literature. Cultural literacy and exposure to great books can guard against aberrations and cultish expressions of Christianity like the church my family attended. Literacy expands our kids' view of the world and decreases the likelihood that they will apply "Bible verse Band-Aids" to harsh realities. Further, kids will have more empathy and better understand human nature. Even time-honored fantasy and fairy tales can make them long for a better world and inspire them to do great deeds.

Additionally, a knowledge of history and tradition can provide perspective when church leaders fall or are exposed. Think David and Bathsheba, Judas' betrayal, or even early church heretics like Marcion or Arius. Marcion's butchered collection of scripture was a catalyst for church-wide consensus on a closed canon—the Bible we have today. Arius, an unwitting father of the Jehovah's Witness

---

[23]Meg Meeker, *Strong Fathers, Strong Daughters* (Washington, DC: Regnery, 2006), 23.

movement, taught that Jesus was a created being distinct from God. His error, however, served a larger and useful purpose in the struggle to clarify the orthodox doctrine of Christ's divinity in relationship to God the Father. This is also an example of how God often uses the distorted to show the beauty of the clear.

Fast forward to the 1400s, a time of great corruption in the Roman Catholic church. For example, Pope Alexander VI, "a wealthy Spaniard who allegedly bought the papacy by bribing his fellow electors. Alexander also saw no problem appointing many of his relatives to positions of power, or killing off rival cardinals to claim their valuable property for himself. And he was apparently quite the ladies' man, fathering several children with his many mistresses."[24] And by the time Luther came on the scene in the early 1500s the church was selling "indulgences," certificates peasants could purchase for a fee to supposedly guarantee their loved ones a reduced time in purgatory. In recent history, there were the Jim Baker and Jimmy Swaggart charlatans whose lies, opulence, and fraud were exposed in the 1980's.

Take-away #4: Commit yourself to the joy and life-long discipline of reading and learning. If you're a parent, make sure this is combined with plenty of physical and emotional closeness to your children.

Pride and the Unhealed Father Wound

Reading and knowledge, however, are not cure-alls, as important as they are. Pride and the father wound produce the greatest vulnerability to the dangers associated with a toxic church. Pride blocks off grace, the prime mover of Christian growth. It is only having humility, that is—seeing yourself as needing help, that makes spiritual healing possible.[25] Spiritual healing also includes healing in the area of family-of-origin wounds. Regrettably, this is vividly illustrated in the story of my father.

---

[24] https://www.cnn.com/2018/04/10/europe/catholic-church-most-controversial-popes/index.html
[25] James 4:6.

My dad suffers from what many call the "father wound." He carries deep, unhealed wounds from a father he feels never understood or accepted him. I believe this is the primary reason he was vulnerable to and threw himself—and his family—into a lethal church environment. His uniqueness, entrepreneurial spirit, energy, and competencies were recognized by the church, which rewarded him with the three essentials for a healthy self-worth: I am accepted, I am valuable, and I am important.[26] His hunger for belonging and relational harmony made him susceptible. He never felt these from his father, and the evidence suggests that he also never came to know the deep love of the Heavenly Father's heart expressed in the cross. British author and theologian Alister McGrath explores the important relationship between the cross and a Christian's self-worth:

> Secular therapies too often…repudiate any sense of personal guilt. In particular, both cognitive therapy and Rogerian therapy seem to minimize the negative personal or individual moral dimensions of the human situation by rejecting ideas such as blame or guilt and the vital, related notion of repentance…. The cross is, and must be, the ultimate ground of Christian confidence [self-worth]…. Through the cross of Christ we are restored to fellowship with our Father God, with all the benefits this brings to us…. That is how much he values us. He gives everything he has and everything he is for us. That thought must allow us to walk tall, secure in the fatherly love of God.[27]

Sadly, on this side of spirituality "wrongly pursued," my dad has chosen a carefully guarded state of disinterest and contempt for all religion. He seems unable to feel the father heart of God, and his experience at Berachah left him with many reasons not to trust

---

[26] Sometimes the message, "I am capable," is included here. It is related to the question, "Do I have what it takes?" As John Eldredge points out in his writings, a message that all fathers should make sure they pass on to their children, especially sons, is "You have what it takes."

[27] Johanna McGrath and Alister McGrath, *Self-esteem: The Cross and Christian Confidence*, (Wheaton, IL: Crossway, 1992).

any love associated with a church. Indeed, his father wound remains intact and unhealed, functioning as an additional barrier to the possibility of peace with God. As N.T. Wright has observed:

> It was—with the distressing predictability that clergy and counsellors know only too well—that deep down in his memory and imagination [the man who cannot believe in or feel the love of God] there was a sense of unlovedness; of family and teachers telling him that he was no good; of never being praised or cherished or celebrated. No doubt there was praise and celebration at various times, But the abiding life-forming memories are of condemnation, criticisms, put-downs. Being made to feel inferior, stupid, weak. So the capacity to receive love, had been covered over as though with a thick, calloused, leathery skin… There's a glorious, beautiful world out there, but some people turn in on themselves, bundling themselves up in darkness to avoid being dazzled.[28]

Take-away #5: Beware—pride and an undiagnosed and unhealed father-wound can make you unable to feel the love of God, as well as make you profoundly blind to dangers that can seriously harm you or your family.

A Weak Marriage and Busyness

I believe these unmet needs in my father also contributed greatly to the dissolution of my parents' marriage. A marriage, even if it is not troubled, can never give a heart what only God can. When we have significant unhealed wounds, we often can't separate legitimate criticism of ourselves (e.g. talking about a specific problem in the relationship) from rejection of our person. And, as many have experienced, it's hard to improve a relationship if the other person interprets your words only through a lens of rejection—a lens that causes them to shut down, never address the problem, and ultimately withdraw from you.

---

[28] N.T. Wright, *Lent for Everyone: Mark, Year B* (Louisville, KY: Westminster John Knox Press, 2012) 85-87.

When your marriage is weak, there's no strength in uniformity—the "one-flesh principal" doesn't work, and you can't talk through heavy topics together. Of course, my parent's marriage was ailing before they went to Berachah but there's no doubt Berachah's "it's your responsibility to save the whole world," real-spiritual-people-are-at-the-church-every-night-of-the-week culture kept them distracted from addressing the pain in their relationship. Added to this, the busyness of starting a new business and Berachah's constant fundraising kept them from financial margin, and many life-giving, shared memories that come from days off, weekend getaways, vacations, and even time with healthy friends.

Take-away #6: Busyness—even in a church culture—kills. Moreover, a healthy marriage and family matter far more to God than church programs. Never join a church that doesn't reinforce this message, and if you're part of one now, leave.

Toxic Leaders

Finally, why did it happen? Because of toxic leaders in a toxic church. In my analysis, this last item must not be minimized. Baby Christians like my mom and dad were vulnerable, as were the already troubled foster children the Jansons took in. Indeed, it's understandable why some people run from the church never to return. Toxic leaders are worthy of blame and will be judged more severely:

- "Dear brothers and sisters, not many of you should become teachers in the church, for we who teach will be judged more strictly."[29]
- "If anyone causes one of these little ones—those who believe in me—to stumble, it would be better for them to have a large millstone hung around their neck and to be drowned in the depths of the sea."[30]

Those of us who love Christ and His church must be honest: The Bible in the wrong hands is like giving a child a chainsaw to

---

[29] James 3:1, NLT.
[30] Matthew 18:6, NIV.

play with his peers. In a scenario like that, there's no way someone will not get seriously injured. Spiritual abuse can cut deeply, just like sexual abuse or the father wound. Further, while the church may keep some people safe from sin, it can also keep them squelched. Their potential is pressed down hard, smashed into a pickle jar, the threads of the lid barely catching. Those who grow up this way become deformed in ways that those looking from the outside can see clearly, and it scares them. They are "Jesus Freaks" in the worst sense of the phrase, collected under one roof with a steeple, and they wonder why folks outside don't want to come in.

For example, a friend who grew up in a similar cult-like environment to Berachah was taken out of figure skating lessons just when she started to get the hang of it. The reason? She was required to wear figure-skating costumes! Even when her instructor explained to her parents that she couldn't wear an ankle-length skirt for safety reasons, it didn't matter. She was forced to stop, and this crushed her spirit. As you can imagine, those watching from the outside thought this was nonsense and were deeply concerned. My friend said she wasn't even allowed to play sports (even on the homeschool teams) because of the uniforms she'd have to wear. Even baggy sleeveless jerseys and loose knee-length shorts were still too immodest!

It's no surprise given the myriad of ridiculous stories like this why some choose to write off the Church and Christianity altogether. And this brings up a fair question related to places like Berachah or the Church as a whole: Should a movement be judged by its abuses?" I first heard Dr. Ravi Zacharias speak to this question during a talk he gave at Harvard University defending the Christian faith. He said, "Don't judge a movement by its abuses" and applied it to some of Christianity's most appalling abuses like the Crusades, Salem witch trials, and racial bigotry and slavery. His point? Don't judge the person and message of Christ, or the center of a good, great, and vast movement by its aberrations or ugliest moments. Put simply, don't throw the baby out with the bathwater.

For example, in recent years, I've enjoyed *Blue Bloods*, the award-winning TV show that gives a fictional and inviting vision of

Irish Catholicism played out in a family of police officers. Conversely, the Oscar-winning film *Spotlight* gives a factual and repulsive account of the widespread child sex abuse by numerous Roman Catholic priests in the Boston area. What are we to think of these disparities? Again, I think Dr. Zacharias' wisdom applies: don't judge a movement (i.e. the Roman Catholic Church as a whole) by its abuses.[31] Analogously, just because counterfeit money exists doesn't mean we stop using currency. Again, Tolstoy made a similar point, applying a "don't judge a movement by its abuses" logic to his own seriously flawed example as a Christian:

> Attack me, I do this myself, but attack me rather than the path I follow and which I point out to anyone who asks me where I think it lies. If I know the way home and am walking along it drunkenly, is it any less the right way because I am staggering from side to side?[32]

Yet, what did Jesus say? "You will recognize them by their fruits."[33] When Jesus said "fruits," he was talking about both the actions of a particular teacher and the legacy that teacher leaves in the lives of his or her followers. How do his words apply to "don't judge a movement by its abuses"? Honestly, like so many things Jesus said, they call for nuance as the "abuses" in question could be one of four areas:

- **"Heresies"**[34] — False Teachings that become

---

[31] On a related note, Rod Dreher, Senior Editor at *The American Conservative*, aptly observed: "Now, it is undeniably true that some of the more fundamentalist forms of Christianity— Catholic, Protestant, and Orthodox— can do serious psychological and emotional damage to people... It's wrong for Christians (or Jews, Muslims, and any other religious believer) to be so defensive about attacks on our faith that we deny that people within the religion can use its teachings to psychologically abuse others. But we should be very wary of attempts to pathologize all orthodox religious belief." Rod Dreher, "Christophobia is Real" in The American Conservative (February 8, 2019). https://www.theamericanconservative.com/dreher/christophobia-is-real/.
[32] Phillip Yancy, *Soul Survivor* (New York: Doubleday, 2001), 130.
[33] Matt. 7:20, ESV.
[34] I am defining heresy here as something the church as a whole over time (based on scriptural authority and tradition rather than simply power) agrees is false and, therefore, harmful.

movements with their associated leader or "heretic." This is "the fringe of the fringe" of a movement like Berachah's or Gothardism.

- **Times when the global church has missed the boat**— Think back to the church's initial response to Galileo and Copernicus' heliocentric view of the known universe.[35] Or think of many of the church's current responses to evolution or related findings from the Human Genome Project.
- **Flawed individual examples who are nevertheless honest** (like Tolstoy). We all have our sins and thankfully there is still hope for our rebel hearts when we look to Christ in faith and repentance. In Isaiah 30:1-17, God's people forsake him for a false salvation and what do we find in 18a? "Therefore the LORD waits to be gracious to you, and therefore he exalts himself to show mercy to you."
- **Blatant misrepresentation and hypocrisy**—Pastor Janson or the pedophile-priests in the movie *Spotlight* provide clear examples of wolves in sheep's clothing. Although this category must sometimes be combined with "heresies" or "heretics", this is not always the case.

Almost forty years later, the best answer I've found to the difficult question, "should a movement be judged by its abuses?" is from Alister McGrath. He gives clarity on what heresy is, how we should view it, as well as the challenge of how it relates to judging a movement by its abuses in light of Jesus' words in Matthew 7:20:

[A Christian heresy is] "best seen as a form of Christian belief that, more by accident than design, ultimately ends up subverting, destabilizing or even destroying the core of Christian faith… [But] both this process of destabilization and the identification of its threat may be spread out over an

---

[35] The heliocentric view refers to the idea that the sun is at the center of the solar system, rather than the earth. "Helio" means sun.

extended period of time."[36]

Still, despite "heresies," flawed individuals, and all the stupid and even heinous stories associated with the Christian faith, for two thousand years the church has lived on with a much larger legacy of spreading literacy, reforming prisons, and millions of other unsung expressions of cultural enrichment, beauty, and grace. Think of the monks and nuns during the middle ages. The late Charles Colson noted that:

> Instead of conforming to the barbarian culture of the Dark Ages, the medieval church modeled a counterculture to a world engulfed by destruction and confusion. Thousands of monastic orders spread across Europe, characterized by discipline, creativity, and a coherence. Monks preserved not only the Scriptures but classical literature as well. They were busy not only at their prayers but in clearing land, building towns, and harvesting crops. When little else shone forth, these religious provided attractive models of communities of caring and character; and in the process they preserved both faith and civilization itself."[37]

Or think of Bach, G.K. Chesterton, and champions of justice and love like William Wilberforce or Mother Teresa. Even in America specifically, as New York Times Columnist Ross Douthat points out:

> From the beginning, the existence of a Christian center… has helped bind together a teeming, diverse… nation. This binding has often been tangible and concrete: The hierarchy, discipline, and institutional continuity of Mainline Protestantism and Catholicism helped build hospitals and schools, orphanages and universities, and assimilated generation upon generation of immigrants. But our religious center has bound us together in a more mysterious fashion as well. In a country without a national church, a kind of 'mere Christianity' has frequently provided a

---

[36] Alister McGrath, *Heresy: A History of Defending the Truth* (New York: Harper Collins, 2009), 11-12.
[37] Charles Colson, *Against the Night* (Ann Arbor, MI: Vine Books, 1989), 132.

kind of invisible mortar for our culture and a common vocabulary for our great debates."[38]

Take-away #7: Don't be naïve, and don't judge the whole of Christianity by its abuses. Wolves and extremism are real and will always be associated with the church. Intelligent, loving leadership teams that cherish Scripture and are trained to handle it correctly are wonderful safeguards against the fake, the freakish, the toxic, and abusers of all kinds.

---

[38] Ross Douthat, *Bad Religion: How We Became a Nation of Heretics* (New York: Free Press, 2012), 7.

CONCLUSION

If it is that you have found a better way indeed, would not wisdom urge you back to where there is a need?
—Greg Austen

The question above came to me rather quickly one day as I was contemplating my dad's abandonment of faith. He taught me to love God and yet he no longer believed in the uniqueness of Christ. Further, to this day, he wants nothing to do with organized religion. I thought he had returned to his agnostic roots, but he says he's now an atheist. Honestly, he seems more like an apatheist. An apatheist is defined as "someone who is not interested in accepting or rejecting any claims that gods exist or do not exist. The existence of god(s) is not rejected, but may be designated irrelevant."[1] I became acquainted with this term through Jim, another former schoolmate and one of Berachah's victims. Like my dad, Jim too has left the faith and considers himself an apatheist.

My dad's answer to the "would not wisdom urge you back" question above was a resounding "no." My answer was "yes" but I've had a hard time figuring out exactly what "back to where there is a need" means. At first, I thought it was about geography. Maybe the struggles Pam and I had gone through growing up in South Jersey uniquely qualified us for ministry there. That was one interpretation and it's probably why I returned briefly and tried to help the senior pastor rebrand Berachah before I went to seminary in 1992. I even left with the idea that one day after seminary I might

---

[1] https://en.wikipedia.org/wiki/Apatheism

well be back in South Jersey to implement my vision of what church could be. Indeed, as I look back at my journals, as early as June 1993, I was making plans to return to the "scene of the crime," this time to put a team together and plant a church in my home county. I even tried to put my hat in the ring when a pastor left an existing church in the area. Nothing, however, ever came of any of these attempts to go "back to where there is a need." Twenty years went by and this dream (or perhaps a wound time would not wash clean) stayed with me.

In November 2011, I lost my position as Senior Director of National Programming at National Fatherhood Initiative (NFI) amid a scourge of layoffs. With seminary long behind me, I had served six years as pastor of a church in Willow Grove, Pennsylvania and then, in 2004, had come on board with NFI to help them pioneer Christian-based programming. By this time, I was working remotely and had returned to Millville, the town Pam and I were born in. Just prior to the layoff, Pam and I had celebrated our 25th wedding anniversary and, during our time away, had decided that we would return to full-time pastoral ministry once we finished launching our three kids. So, when the layoff happened, although I was disappointed to say goodbye to important work and many dear friends, I was excited at what God might have next.

Knowing that nothing captured my heart more than the challenge of church planting in southern New Jersey, Pam threw the idea out there to see how I might respond. When she did, it was like igniting the pilot light on a gas stove, and my passion burst into flame. With her encouragement and buy-in, it now seemed like the planets had aligned and I could finally make the dream a reality.

With our home church's blessing, we began to move forward and in March 2012, went to Mission to North America's Church Planting Assessment Center. After an intensive, three-day evaluation, we were thrilled to be one of the two couples out of six that were fully recommended for church planting. I immediately began to raise funds to supplement a tent-making model of ministry that utilized my carpentry skills.[2] The plan was, then, to officially start church planting work and drawing on designated funds in 2013. In the fall of 2012, after raising close to fifty thousand dollars toward our start, Pam's job in healthcare became extremely stressful, and my carpentry work dried up. This ultimately led, in December 2012, to the painful decision—especially for me—to pull the plug on our plans just before we would have begun to draw on support.

2012 saw both the birth and the death of a twenty-year vision. The year that followed was extremely difficult. I went from grieving a loss to feeling lost, and ended up in a place of disillusionment. Reality bites, and circumstances had brought a very unexpected answer to my question:

"If it is that you have found a better way indeed, would not wisdom urge you back to where there is a need?" Answer?

"Not necessarily."

At least not in the sense that I thought, geographically.

Although it didn't feel like a gift at first, through all the frustration of "my plans," God made it crystal clear that my dream of planting a church in the area I grew up in had been an emotional call, not a divine one. The passion was real but related more to wounds from Berachah and my parents' subsequent divorce, rather than a mission from God. Finally able to put all this behind me, I began to focus on the road ahead, leaning heavily on two quotes that I entered in my journal:

- "Show me the path where I should walk, O LORD; point out the right road for me to follow. Lead me by your truth and teach me, for you are the God who saves me. All day long I put my hope in you."[3]
- "Nothing could be farther from the truth than the... belief that God only manifests himself in progress... Real spiritual

---

[2] A "tent-making" model of ministry is connected to the example of the Apostle Paul (Acts 18:3) who used his trade to provide or partially provide his own financial support, so as not to burden those God had called him to serve.
[3] Psalm 25:4-5.

> progress can only be achieved through catastrophe and suffering, reaching new levels after the profound catharsis which accompanies major upheavals. Every such period of mental and physical agony, while the old is being swept away and the new is still unborn, yields different social patterns and deeper spiritual insights."[4]

A significant chapter in my life had closed, and as this book also concludes, I now pass this crucial prayer and insight on to you. In fact, although this book is dedicated to my parents, its contents were written with you in mind. I pray it helps you pack up some old things, heal, and look to God for new direction. That it shatters any illusion that your suffering is too great for God to bring you to a place of hope. In fact, Scripture reveals that this is *the normal process* God uses to grow his people: "…we rejoice in our sufferings, knowing that suffering produces endurance, and endurance produces character, and character produces hope and hope does not put us to shame, because God's love has been poured into our hearts through the Holy Spirit who has been given to us"[5]

This doesn't mean that suffering is good or that we should seek it out for its own sake. Romans 8:28 is often used glibly to say that bad—even monstrous—things are not that bad because they will work out for good: "For we know that all things work together for good to those who love God…." In context, however, this promise has a narrow focus and should only be interpreted salvifically; that is, connected to what it says about being conformed to the image of Christ. To *not* see this and to connect "all things" to health, wealth or good fortune in any way is a deception associated with the prosperity gospel.[6] Further, to *not* see the narrow focus of this verse sets many up for disillusionment and bitterness toward God, especially when they or their loved ones *don't* end up getting their "best life now."

---

[4] William F. Albright, *From the Stone Age to Christianity: Monotheism and the Historical Process*, 311.
[5] Romans 5:3-5, ESV.
[6] The prosperity gospel is a belief among some Christians that financial blessing and physical well-being are always the will of God for his children.

Here are the verses that follow and make clear the meaning of Romans 8:28:

(28) And we know that all things work together for good to them that love God, to them who are the called according to *his* purpose. (29) For whom he did foreknow, he also did predestinate *to be* conformed to the image of his Son, that he might be the firstborn among many brethren. (30) Moreover whom he did predestinate, them he also called: and whom he called, them he also justified: and whom he justified, them he also glorified.

Three things are important in interpreting Romans 8:28 correctly:

- This promise is only for those that "love God."
- The "his purpose" at the end of 28 is unpacked in 29-30: whom he **foreknew**, he **predestined**, whom he predestined, he **called**, whom he called he **justified**, and whom he justified he **glorified**. These five rich theological concepts represent the chronological unfolding of "his purpose" from a human perspective.
- The actual point or goal of this whole process is sandwiched right smack in the middle of the five terms: becoming like Jesus. In other words, "his purpose" is "to be conformed to the image of his Son." *That* is the "good" all things are working together for in verse 28.

And this is the same "hope" that is also at the end of the process in Romans 5:5 above. Moreover, the application of both passages taken together is one of the greatest encouragements of this book and I pray you don't miss it:

If you love God, he will use even the ugliest, most painful experiences in your life to make you more like Jesus. What's more, he'll lovingly shape you into the image of Christ in such a way that, more and more, you'll become a conduit of his holy love.

This is Hope with a capital H and a promise worthy of our full confidence! God is the trustworthy parent who, like my mom at Bushkill's treacherous falls, holds our hand through even the most hurtful and terrible events in our lives.[7] What's more, as the conclusion of Romans 8 says, nothing can separate us from his love:

> And I am convinced that nothing can ever separate us from God's love. Neither death nor life, neither angels nor demons, neither our fears for today nor our worries about tomorrow—not even the powers of hell can separate us from God's love. No power in the sky above or in the earth below—indeed, nothing in all creation will ever be able to separate us from the love of God that is revealed in Christ Jesus our Lord.[8]

In the last seven years as I've completed my doctorate, done seminars on *The Dangers of Growing Up in a Christian Home (and how to avoid them!)*, and started writing a weekly blog at carpentertheologian.com, God has shown me that the answer to my question ultimately had nothing to do with a physical location like South Jersey. It's rather about joining myself with Jesus' purposes—something directly in sync with this insight from Erwin McManus:

> Sometimes your future will call you to stand right in the middle of your past. The difference, of course, is that you are not defined by the past, enslaved by the past, or held captive by it. Sometimes the only way to set people free from the past is to create a different future that gives all those around you the inspiration and hope to set their own past free.[9]

And that's what my story, *How I Became a Christian Despite the Church*, is all about: standing in the middle of *my* past to set *you* free, to create a different future that gives you inspiration and hope to set your own past free. It's about giving you a clear path to "genuine faith," and doing so in such a way that your "faith continues strong."[10] I've come to see that "back to where there is a need" is ultimately an adventure into the unknown and is about others, not me.

And so, I leave you with any "better way" I've found, as well as

---

[7] Psalm 73:23.
[8] Romans 8:38-39, NLT. Words in bold, mine.
[9] Erwin Rahael McManus, *The Last Arrow: Save Nothing for the Next Life* (New York: Watermark, 2017), 52-53.
[10] 2 Timothy 1:5.

my question that's now for you to answer:

If it is that you have found a better way indeed, would not wisdom urge you back to where there is a need?

May his loving heart lead you into all it means for you and those you love.

APPENDIX 1: FOR THE ROAD

"One of the great sorrows of our age is that people even inside the church, let alone outside of it, have so reacted against the over-dogmatic claims of some 'conservative' Christians concerning the literal truth of the whole Bible (when a great deal is manifestly poetry, and so on), that whole idea of the Bible itself as 'God's word' is discounted by many."[1]
—N.T. Wright

I remember being in Bible college and my professor said, in the context of defending his ultra-dispensational interpretation of Revelation: "If the plain sense of Scripture makes common sense, seek no other sense or you will have nonsense." It was cute, sticky—I still remember it, and it helped me understand his viewpoint but, thankfully, it didn't help me embrace it.

A lot of Christians come at the Bible with this overly-literalistic, treat-Scripture-like-a-newspaper perspective, and when this gets mixed with religious fervor and commitment, things can get scary and ugly. It's because of literal statements in Scripture that many view Christianity as untenable or dangerous. I understand this and, if you've stayed with my story up to this point, you should too. Always taking the Bible literally, especially when one simultaneously devalues theological education, mainstream science, and a thorough knowledge of the Old Testament, ancient Near Eastern and first-century culture is a recipe for spiritual abuse and malpractice.

---

[1] *Lent for Everyone: Mark, Year B* (Louisville, KY: Westminster John Knox Press, 2012), 113.

My goal in this final offering is not to disparage God, the Christian faith, or the Bible. Quite the opposite. It's to encourage you to love God with your mind, abandon unnecessary fences, and silly and/or false views that are unworthy of God. The late Bruce Metzger, one of the foremost NT Scholars of the last century, said it well: "The Bible doesn't always mean what it literally says but it always means what is literally means."

The lists below in no way represent the "best" Christian reading there is. Nor are they meant to be comprehensive or the final word on any subject. What follows represents only those distinctively Christian books and related resources I've found to be the most helpful to date.[2] It's my hope that one or more of these recommendations builds up your faith, answers your questions, and blesses those you love.

Favorites from a Reformed Perspective[3]

- *The Prodigal God* by Tim Keller—this book more than any other has helped me get the gospel; at one time, it was going to be the fire I built a church planting team around.
- *Approaching God* by Steve Brown—the most accessible book on prayer I've found; great stories and shared easily with family.
- *The Disciplines of Grace* by Jerry Bridges—my favorite book on sanctification (growing in Christ); especially helpful is his early description of the "good day/bad day" scenarios and how these affect our relationship with God.

---

[2] This does not mean, however, that I agree with every word in every book or presentation.

[3] These days I take a broad view of what it means to be "Reformed": to seek the honor and glory of God with a special nod to how Calvin, Luther, and other church "Reformers" five hundred years ago recovered and enhanced a helpful (although certainly not perfect) articulation of the biblical tradition in the areas of justification by grace through faith, the sovereignty of God, the primacy of Christ, preaching, scripture, and the sacraments of baptism and the Lord's Supper. I like the term *prima* scriptura rather than *sola* scriptura as I affirm *first of all* what the Bible teaches rather than *only* what the Bible teaches.

- *The Life You Always Wanted* by John Ortberg— a lighter read but extremely accessible and practical; Ortberg is a great communicator and this is my second favorite on sanctification.
- *The Scandal of the Evangelical Mind* by Mark Noll—Noll champions loving God with our minds and I especially love his chapter on "Thinking About Science."
- *To Be Near Unto God* by Abraham Kuyper—probably my favorite devotional; a great mix of head and heart, although a little heavy for simple bathroom reading.
- *The Mystery of the Holy Spirit* by R.C. Sproul—Sproul was a great communicator and teacher; contains a very helpful chapter on the Baptism of the Holy Spirit.
- *The Body* by Charles Colson
- *Adventures in Evangelical Civility* by Richard Mouw
- *Discovering God's Will* by Sinclair Fergusen—I read this when I was twenty and it's still my favorite on the topic; the chapters on "Choosing a Spouse" and Vocation are especially helpful.
- *The Five Points of Calvinism: Documented, Defended, and Defined* by Steele and Thomas—thorough with loads of Scripture; helped me early in my faith journey to understand and embrace the doctrines of grace.
- *Calvinism and the Las Vegas Airport* by Richard Mouw—Mouw is one of my favorite writers and this book talks honestly about some of the hard edges of Calvinism in a winsome way.
- *Spiritual Depression* by Martyn Lloyd Jones—a collection of sermons to think about spirituality holistically; the first chapter is worth the price of the book; also a great book to read on Sundays (e.g. a chapter each week).
- *Knowing God* by J.I. Packer—a classic to remind us of what is most important and give sound guidance to begin meditating and cultivating a relationship with God for life.

- *That's a Great Question* by R.C. Sproul
- Wayne Grudem's *Systematic Theology*—clear, objective, and thorough; his discussions on the limited atonement, dispensationalism, and especially what those who practice believer's baptism have in common with those practice infant baptism are very valuable.
- *Essentials in Evangelical Theology* by Donald Bloesch—excellent sections on "holy love" as the essence God, understanding his wrath in relation to this, and eschatology.
- *The ESV Study Bible*—If I could only have one book on a desert island, this would be it; best study Bible with notes edited by some of the finest evangelical scholars; replaces 50-100 books in my library.

Other Favorites

- *Mere Christianity* by C.S. Lewis
- *The Unknown God* by Alister McGrath
- *Soul Survivor: How My Faith Survived the Church* by Phillip Yancey
- *Church: Why Bother?* by Phillip Yancey
- *Released from Shame* by Sandra Wilson—especially a chapter called "Released from Shame-based Concepts of God and Religion."
- *Emotionally Healthy Spirituality* and *The Emotionally Healthy Leader* by Pete Scazzero; he also has a course for churches and many excellent podcasts that you can find at https://www.emotionallyhealthy.org/podcast/?v=7516fd43adaa
- *Self-Esteem: The Cross and Christian Confidence* by Joanna and Alister McGrath
- *Desiring the Kingdom* by James K.A. Smith
- *Leading with a Limp: Turning Your Struggles into Strengths* by Dan Allender
- *The Art of Pastoring: Ministry Without All the Answers* by David

Hansen
- *Traveling Mercies* by Anne Lamott
- *Wild at Heart* by John Eldredge—offers a provocative lens for men on what it means to be created in the image of God that he illustrates with movies; excellent chapter on Satan's strategy.
- *Authentic Christianity*—select quotes from the writings of John Stott
- *Scripture and the Authority of God* by N.T. Wright
- *Seriously Dangerous Religion: What the Old Testament Really Says and Why It Matters* by Ian Provan

Genesis 1 and Science:

- *The Lost World of Genesis One* (IVP Academic, 2009) by John Walton—essential for understanding Genesis in the context of other ancient cosmologies, as well as the meaning of the seventh day.
- https://www.christianitytoday.com/ct/2011/june/historicaladam.html—great intro and overview of the science, key advocates, and issues at stake.
- *How I Changed my Mind about Evolution* (Biologos and IVP Academic, 2006)—the title is deceiving as this book is less about evolution and more about wonder, awe, and humility.
- https://biologos.org/blogs/archive/creation-evolution-and-christian-laypeople-part-6—Tim Keller's take on Adam and Eve in view of evolutionary creationism.
- Biologos.org—"BioLogos invites the church and the world to see the harmony between science and biblical faith as we present an evolutionary understanding of God's creation."
- *Coming to Peace with Science* (IVP Academic, 2004) by Darrel Falk—professor of biology explains the evidence for evolution in a very accessible way amidst rich devotional insight.
- *Adam and the Genome* (Brazos, 2017) by Dennis Venema and

Scott McKnight—advanced one of the most comprehensive in explaining both science and ANE documents.
- Denis Lamoureux's PowerPoint presentations on biblical genealogies in which he deals with their nature and connection to Adam as a literal/non-literal person in history: http://www.ualberta.ca/~dlamoure/wlgen1/index.html
- *Did Adam and Eve Really Exist?* (Crossway, 2011) by John Collins

Other Tough Topics

- *When God Weeps: Why Our Sufferings Matter to the Almighty* by Steve Estes and Joni Erickson Tada—wrestles honestly with the problem of pain; wades deep into the hard questions and theological weeds.
- *More Than One Way? Four Views of Salvation in a Pluralistic World* edited by Dennis L. Okholm and Timothy R. Phillips
- *Four Views on Hell* edited by William Crockett
- *Did God Really Command Genocide?: Coming to Terms with the Justice of God* by Paul Copan
- "The Biblical Basis for Women's Service in Church" by N.T.Wright: http://www2.cbeinternational.org/CBE_InfoPack/pdf_files/wright_biblical_basis.pdf
- LGBTQ+:
    - *Washed and Waiting* by Wesly Hill
    - Hour-long interview and testimony of Rosaria Butterfield (includes an excellent Q&A): https://www.youtube.com/watch?v=kQ_YI6INTQU&feature=youtu.be

Favorite Commentaries

- *Genesis: A Commentary* by Bruce Waltke

- *Living Life Backward: How Ecclesiastes Teaches Us To Live in Light of the End* by David Gibson
- *Ecclesiastes, Song of Songs* by Ian Provan (part of The NIV Application series)
- *Breaking the Code*: a commentary on Revelation by Bruce Metzger
- To keep up with the best commentaries available, I use the latest editions of *Old Testament Commentary Survey* by Tremper Longman III and *New Testament Commentary Survey* by D.A. Carson. These are available through Baker Academic.

APPENDIX 2: How I Became a Christian Despite the Church Playlist

"If one happened to consult the pages of some poet, who was singing (and thinking) of quite other matters, the eye often fell on the verse quite extraordinarily relevant to the matter in one's own mind."[1]
—Saint Augustine (354-430 AD)

Martin Luther once said that music was "the handmaiden of theology." In synch with that, I hope that the following eclectic playlist not only aides in your own healing journey but also reinforces the best concepts in this book. The list represents three hours of music: all the songs mentioned in the book mostly in order—plus a few additional ones that seemed "quite extraordinarily relevant" to the topics at hand. Enjoy!

"There Is a River," Michael English
"The River," Dan Fogelberg
"Morning Has Broken," Cat Stevens
"Brother Love's Travelling Salvation Show," Neil Diamond
"Jesus He Knows Me," Genesis
"Bullet The Blue Sky," U2
"Tiny Dancer," Elton John
"Ships," Barry Manilow

---

[1] Augustine, *Confessions,* Second Edition translated by F.J. Sheed (Indianapolis, IN: Hackett Publishing Co., Inc., 2006), 58.

Mozart's The Marriage Of Figaro, K 592 – Overture, performed by the Royal Danish Orchestra
"Wild World," Cat Stevens
"Star Wars (Main Theme)," composed by John Williams and performed by the London Symphony Orchestra
"Kodachrome," Paul Simon
"Oh Father (Alternate Version)," Madonna
"The Time It Is Today," The Association
"My Life," Billy Joel
"I Got a Name," Jim Croce
"Everyday Is A Winding Road," Sheryl Crow
"To Forgive," Steve Taylor
"Beyond Justice to Mercy," Susan Ashton
"Joseph's Trouble," Wes King
"Come In From The Cold," Joni Mitchell
"Under the Rug," Randy Stonehill
"Monkeys At The Zoo," Charlie Peacock
"Until That Final Day," Keith Green
"Grace By Which I Stand," Keith Green
"The History In Your Eyes," Randy Stonehill
"Untouched By Human Hands," Wayne Watson
"Round And Round," Kim Hill
"Love Is All," The Tallest Man On Earth
"Chasing Shadows," Kansas
"Wedding Song (There Is Love)," Paul Stookey
"The Prodigal Son Suite," Keith Green
"Going Home," David Meece
"Where the Light Shines Through," Switchfoot
"Praise the Lord," Crowder
"Old Clothes," Randy Stonehill
"So Will I (100 Billion X)," Hillsong UNITED

APPENDIX 3: Small Group Discussion Questions

"A man[1] doesn't really know himself until he can articulate his thoughts and feelings to a friend."
–Unknown

Small groups have so many benefits and the quote above highlights just one of them: greater self-awareness comes simply as we struggle to get our thoughts and feelings out to a trusted friend. Below is a plan and set of discussion questions for an eleven-week small group. Feel free to modify the questions (or add better ones) based on the needs of your group. The first question under each chapter heading is purposely designed to be a lighter, get-to-know, discussion-starter. I'd also suggest you add the page number in the book that corresponds to each question ahead of time 1) for your group's easy access and 2) so you can easily read a section that gives context to the question if desired.[2]

Introduction

- Read through the introduction together during this first week. Consider taking turns reading each paragraph. Tell any that don't feel comfortable reading out loud to just tap

---

[1] "Man" is used here in its generic sense and refers to any human, male or female.
[2] I would have done this for you but was afraid the pages numbers might be inaccurate by the time it went to press.

the person next to them.
- Introduce Greg's playlist in Appendix #1. Encourage any who desire to find a way to listen to it over the course of the next eleven weeks. Additionally, challenge each person to consider making their own "spiritual journey playlist." Tell them you'll remind them toward the end of the group to complete and share their lists.

Chapter One: A River Ran Through It

- Which of your parents or grandparents did you know best? Which were you closest to? Which had the most influence on you spiritually and why?
- Are you proud of the town you grew up in? Why or why not?
- What stood out to you the most in this chapter? What was the most helpful thing you learned?
- In the thinking about the "Double Helix of Faith and Family," which has been more primary for you: faith or family? Why? Or, how have they worked together?
- Use this question only if you have a lot of parents in the group: In thinking about the three roles of good parents mentioned, which do you find the most challenging? Why?

Chapter Two: God Versus the Boulevard

- This chapter references a lot of things related to culture: music, books, movies, etc. What were your favorites growing up? What about now?
- This chapter also referenced a lot of quotes from the Bible. Which was the most helpful? Which was the hardest to understand?
- Greg says, "Christians have a strange proclivity to fashion Jesus' teaching on the narrow way into a joyless pursuit that devalues creation and makes the world he created very small." What does he mean, and do you agree or disagree?

Why and can you give an example?
- What is your answer to the question: "How do individuals and Christian families live in the world or this culture without becoming part of it?" Which verse or passage of scripture provides insight in answering this question?

Chapter Three: Shame, Distortions, and Abuse

- What thoughts or memories did this chapter trigger that you don't mind sharing?
- Which story did you find the most ridiculous? Which made you the angriest? Which could you relate to the most?
- What is your personal view of discipline and spanking? Do you agree or disagree with Greg? Why? What do you think of the three insights related to a "gentler approach to discipline"?
- At the end of the chapter, Rachael Joy Denhollander says, "Christians don't do well… acknowledging the devastation of the wound." Why do you think that is? What could be done to help change this?

Chapter Four: Breaking Free

- What stood out to you the most in this chapter? What was the most helpful thing you learned?
- Read Romans 2:4 together. Have there been any times in your life, like Greg's story about Maria, where God's goodness led you to repentance?
- In *David Copperfield*, the main character says, "…the best steel must go through the fire…" and essentially asks, "Will I be the hero of my own life or the victim of it?" What "fire" have you been through that has produced "best steel" in your life? In thinking about David's question, do you see yourself as more "hero" or "victim"? Why?
- Greg mentioned that "heart-to-heart friendship really started with my dad's empathy and decision to trust me with

how he really felt." When have you experienced something like that? Do those closest to you experience this from you? Explain.
- Read Hebrews 13:17 together. This can be a scary verse against the backdrop of something like the Jonestown massacre. In this season of your life, how do you feel about "church authority" and commitment to a local church? If you're a Christian, how does Hebrews 10:24-25 inform your thoughts?

Chapter Five: Healing Moves

- Use the following if you have a lot of couples in the group (if not, go to the next question): Greg talks early in this chapter about how he met his wife, Pam. Tell us about how you met your friend, partner, or spouse.
- What is your first memory of being disillusioned by someone you looked up to?
- Sorting through legitimate vs. illegitimate shame can be such a tangled, difficult issue. Were there any insights in Greg's section on shame that stood out to you? Are there any passages of Scripture that that have been especially helpful in this area?
- Do you have anyone in your life that you've forgiven but haven't and/or have no interest in reconciling with? If you're willing, talk about that.
- Greg lists a few questions that helped him evaluate his heart and work toward forgiveness. Which one(s) do you find the most helpful?
- What phrase stands out to you the most in Wes King's song "Joseph's Trouble" as the end of the chapter? Why?

Chapter Six: Sexual Staggers

- We definitely live in a sexually saturated culture. That being the case, do you think the church talks too little or too much

about sex? What are the challenges if a church decides to be more intentional in addressing sexually "hot topics"?
- In thinking about the five strategies for fighting lust, which did you resonate with as a way to fight lust or any other sin?
- Use the following if you have a lot of middle-aged couples in the group (if not, go to the next question): In Greg's nine strategies for navigating mid-life and the empty nest years which one is a good word for you right now?
- Do you agree with John White's caution against using Matthew 5:28 as a primary apologetic against pornography? Why or why not? Is there anything you would add to Greg's statement toward the end of the chapter about why pornography is wrong? What scripture(s) have you found helpful in guarding your heart in this area?
- Read Isaiah 30:15 that's mentioned together. Thinking beyond the topic of sex, how does this verse apply in your life right now?

Chapter Seven: Learning to Love

- Right at the beginning of the chapter, Greg mentions how impactful Randy Stonehill's lyric has been in guiding and making sense of his journey. Are there any songs or movies that have been especially meaningful to you in your spiritual journey?
- Greg mentions a poster he had of Nadia Comaneci on a balance beam with this phrase under it: "Don't pray for an easy life; pray to be a strong person." Read Psalm 46:1-7 together. How has God been a refuge and strength to you in the past? How is he one now?
- Greg discusses shame-based vs. grace-based churches. What has been your experience with either one of these?
- Use this question only if you have a lot of parents in the group: How has God used your kids to teach you about love?

- In thinking about the phrase "God is love" and how it relates to hell and God's wrath, were either Donald Bloesch's or N.T. Wright's insights helpful in how you view God? If so, how?

Chapter Eight: Finding God

- What do you think about C.S. Lewis' interesting quote about nature and the existence of God? What examples could be given to illustrate his point?
- Greg said that fatherhood especially has provided him with powerful evidence of a loving Creator. What about you? What informs your view of what God is like?
- Read John 14:6. Do you believe that Jesus is the way, the truth, and the life? If so, why? If not, what are your barriers to doing so?
- In 1 Corinthians 15, the apostle Paul makes a solid case for the concept of resurrection and the reality of the resurrection of Jesus Christ. Which of Paul's arguments that Greg details do you find the most compelling?
- Greg says, "When it comes to faith, grace is essential" and then quotes Bono. Why is grace such a foundational concept in Christianity? How would you support your view from the Bible?

Chapter Nine: Why It Happened

- Which of the seven reasons or associated "lessons learned" was the most helpful to you in this chapter? Why?
- Read Acts 17:11 and Hebrews 5:11-14 together. Greg lists five characteristics of biblical discipleship taken from these passages. Which is your favorite and which (if any) do you think needs greater emphasis today?
- Greg says "pride and the father wound produce the greatest vulnerability to the dangers associated with a toxic church." Do you agree or disagree? Why? If you disagree, what would

you say instead?
- ***Remind those who have not done so already (and still desire to do so) to bring their playlist to share on the final week of class.

Conclusion

- What does Greg's question "If it is that you have learned a better way indeed, would not wisdom urge you back to where there is a need?" mean for you? Does it apply at all or not? Why or why not?
- Read Romans 8:28-39 and then read the section in the book about how the full context of Romans 8 helps us get verse 28 right. Share your insights on why this section is so important.
- If you have time, have each person share their greatest insight from the book as a whole.

Acknowledgements

As I mentioned in chapter 9, humility is "seeing yourself as needing help," and some of us need that help more than others!

That said, I'm extremely grateful to the following friends and family for either their research, edits, or valuable feedback on this project: Pam Austen, Lois Hart, Tim & Sarah Austen, Josh & Emily Ginchereau, Susan Bukosky, Jennifer Gerelds, Ardee Coolidge, Roland Warren, Gordon Fish, Darrell Proctor, Andrew Smith, Ken Larter, Alli Nielsen, Eve Gleason, Vince DiCaro, Gary Springer, Andrew Larson, Amy Scherschligt, Heather Creekmore, Amy Ford, Jeanneane Maxon, Enno Jurisson, and Paul Waller.

About the Author

Dr. Greg Austen

Greg is Executive Director of Church Outreach & Engagement for Care Net. Before coming to Care Net, Greg worked for National Fatherhood Initiative and as a pastor in New Jersey, Kentucky, and Pennsylvania. A seasoned communicator and community strategist, Greg is a licensed teaching elder in the Evangelical Presbyterian Church (EPC). Greg holds a D.Min. from Westminster Theological Seminary, an M.Div. from Southern Seminary, and a B.S. from Cairn University.

Greg writes a weekly blog at carpentertheologian.com and lives in the Greater Philadelphia area with his wife of thirty-three years, Pam. Together they have three married children and four grandchildren.

A few of Greg's favorite things are exploring new places with Pam, spending time with his kids and grandkids, and a quiet morning with a book and a good cup of fresh ground coffee.

Made in the USA
Coppell, TX
20 April 2020